January 2022

Heights: metres (above chart datum)

Times GMT / BST

Date	Day	Moon	WINTERTON HW AM	WINTERTON HW PM	WINTERTON LW AM	WINTERTON LW PM	GORLESTON HW AM	GORLESTON LW AM	GORLESTON HW PM	GORLESTON LW PM	WELLS BAR HW AM	WELLS BAR HW PM
1	Sat		05:11 3.4	17:58 3.3		12:25 0.8	07:07 2.6	01:01 0.6	19:52 2.4	13:33 0.6	04:17 5.6	16:57 5.6
2	Sun	●	06:15 3.5	18:46 3.4	00:54 1.0	13:20 0.8	08:03 2.6	01:58 0.8	20:37 2.6	14:22 0.7	05:19 5.8	17:47 5.8
3	Mon		07:18 3.6	19:34 3.6	01:53 0.8	14:11 0.9	09:06 2.6	02:59 0.7	21:24 2.6	15:12 0.7	06:16 5.9	18:34 6.0
4	Tue		08:15 3.6	20:19 3.7	02:48 0.8	14:59 0.9	10:09 2.6	03:56 0.5	22:11 2.7	16:02 0.8	07:08 6.0	19:19 6.0
5	Wed		09:06 3.5	21:04 3.7	03:38 0.5	15:45 1.1	11:05 2.6	04:48 0.4	22:59 2.8	16:49 0.9	07:59 6.0	20:03 6.0
6	Thu		09:54 3.3	21:47 3.7	04:26 0.4	16:29 1.1	11:55 2.5	05:37 0.4	23:46 2.8	17:33 1.0	08:48 5.8	20:47 5.9
7	Fri		10:43 3.1	22:30 3.6	05:13 0.5	17:11 1.3		06:25 0.4	12:44 2.4	18:16 1.1	09:36 5.5	21:30 5.8
8	Sat		11:35 2.9	23:13 3.4	06:00 0.6	17:55 1.4	00:33 2.7	07:12 0.5	13:33 2.2	19:00 1.1	10:24 5.3	22:15 5.6
9	Sun	◑		12:35 2.7	06:49 0.7	18:42 1.5	01:20 2.7	08:02 0.6	14:25 2.2	19:45 1.3	11:15 5.0	23:04 5.3
10	Mon		00:01 3.2	13:46 2.6	07:43 0.9	19:38 1.6	02:09 2.6	08:55 0.8	15:25 2.1	20:37 1.4		12:14 4.8
11	Tue		00:58 3.0	14:53 2.6	08:46 1.1	20:50 1.6	03:02 2.4	09:54 0.9	16:35 2.1	21:42 1.4	00:02 5.0	13:17 4.7
12	Wed		02:10 2.9	15:57 2.7	09:53 1.2	22:11 1.6	04:00 2.3	10:55 1.0	17:38 2.2	23:02 1.4		
13	Thu		03:26 2.8	16:53 2.8	10:53 1.2	23:17 1.4	05:06 2.3	11:52 1.0	18:30 2.2			
14	Fri		04:52 2.8	17:37 2.9	11:43 1.1		06:09 2.2	00:18 1.2	19:15 2.3	12:41 1.0		
15	Sat		05:55 2.8	18:14 3.0	00:11 1.3	12:25 1.2	07:09 2.2	01:18 1.1	19:50 2.4	13:21 1.0		
16	Sun		06:40 2.9	18:44 3.2	00:57 1.2	13:00 1.2	08:05 2.2	02:04 1.0	20:11 2.4	13:51 1.0		
17	Mon	○	07:19 2.9	19:13 3.3	01:38 1.0	13:31 1.2	09:00 2.3	02:42 0.9	20:27 2.5	14:18 1.0		
18	Tue		07:54 3.0	19:44 3.4	02:17 0.9	14:00 1.2	09:33 2.3	03:16 0.8	20:59 2.6	14:50 0.9		
19	Wed		08:26 3.0	20:17 3.4	02:54 0.8	14:33 1.1	10:16 2.3	03:50 0.7	21:39 2.6	15:28 0.9		
20	Thu		08:59 3.0	20:51 3.5	03:32 0.8	15:09 1.1	11:01 2.3	04:27 0.6	22:24 2.6	16:09 0.9		
21	Fri		09:32 2.9	21:26 3.5	04:09 0.8	15:46 1.1	11:45 2.3	05:06 0.6	23:08 2.6	16:50 0.9		
22	Sat		10:07 2.9	22:01 3.4	04:47 0.7	16:23 1.2	12:30 2.2	05:48 0.6	23:52 2.6	17:31 0.9		
23	Sun		10:45 2.8	22:39 3.4	05:26 0.8	17:03 1.2		06:30 0.6	12:30 2.2	18:12 1.0		
24	Mon		11:28 2.8	23:19 3.3	06:06 0.8	17:48 1.3	00:35 2.6	07:16 0.7	13:18 2.2	18:54 1.1		
25	Tue	◐		12:21 2.6	06:53 0.8	18:42 1.4	01:18 2.5	08:06 0.8	14:12 2.1	19:44 1.1		
26	Wed		00:10 3.2	13:27 2.6	07:48 0.9	19:50 1.4	02:03 2.4	09:06 0.8	15:22 2.1	20:53 1.2		
27	Thu		01:18 3.2	14:41 2.7	08:55 1.0	21:11 1.4	03:00 2.4	10:14 0.9	16:42 2.1	22:26 1.2		
28	Fri		02:41 3.1	15:44 2.8	10:05 1.0	22:30 1.3	04:39 2.4	11:20 0.9	17:46 2.2	23:42 1.1		
29	Sat		03:54 3.1	16:45 2.9	11:11 1.0	23:43 1.1	05:57 2.4		18:39 2.3	12:19 0.9		
30	Sun		05:08 3.2	17:42 3.1		12:13 1.0	07:03 2.4	00:51 0.9	19:28 2.4	13:14 0.9		
31	Mon		06:25 3.3	18:34 3.3	00:53 0.9	13:11 1.0	08:14 2.4	01:58 0.7	20:15 2.5	14:10 0.9		

Tidal information computed by POLTIPS software developed by National Oceanography Centre

February 2022

Times: GMT / BST

Heights: metres (above chart datum)

Day		Moon	HUNSTANTON HW AM		HW PM		LW AM		LW PM		CROMER/SHERINGHAM HW AM		HW PM		LW AM		LW PM		BLAKENEY BAR HW AM		HW PM	
1	Tue	●	06:27	6.8	18:33	6.9	00:54	0.9	13:09	1.0	06:33	4.9	18:38	5.0	00:54	0.8	13:07	1.0	06:23	5.5	18:30	5.6
2	Wed		07:18	7.0	19:16	7.1	01:51	0.5	13:58	0.9	07:21	5.0	19:21	5.2	01:55	0.6	13:54	0.9	07:10	5.6	19:12	5.8
3	Thu		08:02	7.0	19:55	7.1	02:41	0.3	14:40	0.9	08:05	5.0	20:01	5.2	02:48	0.5	14:36	0.9	07:54	5.6	19:52	5.8
4	Fri		08:42	6.9	20:33	7.1	03:23	0.2	15:15	1.0	08:46	4.8	20:39	5.2	03:33	0.5	15:13	1.0	08:36	5.5	20:33	5.8
5	Sat		09:19	6.6	21:10	6.9	04:00	0.4	15:46	1.1	09:24	4.6	21:18	5.1	04:10	0.6	15:48	1.1	09:15	5.3	21:12	5.6
6	Sun		09:56	6.3	21:50	6.6	04:33	0.8	16:15	1.4	10:03	4.4	21:59	4.8	04:42	0.8	16:23	1.3	09:52	5.1	21:51	5.4
7	Mon		10:34	5.9	22:33	6.2	05:03	1.2	16:48	1.6	10:42	4.2	22:43	4.6	05:12	1.1	17:00	1.5	10:30	4.8	22:33	5.1
8	Tue	◐	11:18	5.5	23:24	5.7	05:34	1.6	17:27	2.0	11:29	4.0	23:37	4.2	05:45	1.4	17:43	1.8	11:12	4.6	23:20	4.8
9	Wed				12:12	5.2	06:13	2.1	18:21	2.3			12:28	3.8	06:29	1.7	18:41	2.0			12:04	4.3
10	Thu		00:31	5.3	13:24	5.0	07:08	2.4	19:33	2.6	00:52	3.9	13:47	3.7	07:30	2.0	20:02	2.2	00:23	4.4	13:17	4.2
11	Fri		01:57	5.3	14:45	5.1	08:21	2.5	21:00	2.5	02:24	3.8	15:05	3.7	08:54	2.1	21:35	2.1	01:50	4.2	14:42	4.2
12	Sat		03:19	5.2	15:51	5.3	09:33	2.4	22:11	2.1	03:41	3.8	16:07	3.9	10:09	2.0	22:44	1.8	03:20	4.3	15:54	4.4
13	Sun		04:23	5.4	16:40	5.7	10:30	2.2	23:08	2.0	04:39	4.0	16:55	4.2	11:03	1.8	23:36	1.6	04:25	4.5	16:44	4.7
14	Mon		05:13	5.8	17:21	6.0	11:18	1.8			05:24	4.2	17:35	4.4	11:46	1.6			05:13	4.7	17:24	5.0
15	Tue		05:57	6.1	17:57	6.3	00:00	1.6	12:06	1.5	06:01	4.4	18:09	4.6	00:19	1.3	12:25	1.4	05:51	5.0	17:59	5.2
16	Wed	○	06:36	6.4	18:30	6.6	00:51	1.3	12:51	1.3	06:34	4.5	18:41	4.8	01:00	1.1	13:02	1.2	06:26	5.1	18:32	5.4
17	Thu		07:12	6.6	19:02	6.8	01:36	1.0	13:35	1.1	07:08	4.7	19:12	4.9	01:39	0.9	13:37	1.1	06:58	5.2	19:04	5.5
18	Fri		07:45	6.7	19:33	6.9	02:19	0.8	14:15	1.0	07:42	4.8	19:42	5.0	02:15	0.8	14:12	1.0	07:31	5.4	19:37	5.6
19	Sat		08:16	6.7	20:04	7.0	02:57	0.7	14:52	1.0	08:17	4.8	20:14	5.0	02:51	0.7	14:45	1.0	08:04	5.4	20:10	5.7
20	Sun		08:48	6.6	20:38	7.0	03:32	0.7	15:26	1.1	08:53	4.8	20:47	5.0	03:22	0.7	15:18	1.0	08:39	5.4	20:44	5.6
21	Mon		09:20	6.5	21:16	6.8	04:04	0.8	15:57	1.2	09:30	4.7	21:24	5.0	03:53	0.8	15:51	1.1	09:15	5.3	21:21	5.5
22	Tue		09:57	6.2	22:00	6.6	04:34	1.0	16:29	1.4	10:09	4.5	22:08	4.8	04:25	0.9	16:27	1.2	09:53	5.1	22:02	5.4
23	Wed	●	10:42	5.9	22:55	6.2	05:07	1.3	17:09	1.7	10:54	4.3	23:03	4.6	05:03	1.1	17:12	1.4	10:36	4.9	22:51	5.1
24	Thu		11:39	5.6			05:50	1.6	18:03	2.0	11:51	4.1			05:54	1.4	18:12	1.6	11:33	4.6	23:57	4.8
25	Fri		00:06	5.6	12:57	5.4	06:51	2.0	19:21	2.2	00:15	4.3	13:07	3.9	07:03	1.7	19:33	1.8			12:47	4.5
26	Sat		01:40	5.5	14:27	5.4	08:20	2.1	21:06	2.0	01:55	4.1	14:39	4.0	08:38	1.8	21:14	1.7	01:30	4.6	14:20	4.5
27	Sun		03:17	5.6	15:45	5.8	09:52	2.0	22:39	1.6	03:33	4.2	15:56	4.2	10:09	1.7	22:43	1.4	03:14	4.6	15:46	4.7
28	Mon		04:33	6.0	16:46	6.2	11:07	1.7	23:54	1.1	04:45	4.4	16:55	4.5	11:15	1.5	23:54	1.0	04:34	5.0	16:47	5.0

Tidal information computed by POLTIPS software developed by National Oceanography Centre

Day		WINTERTON HW AM	HW PM	LW AM	LW PM	GORLESTON HW AM	HW PM	LW AM	LW PM	WELLS BAR HW AM	HW PM
1 Tue	●	07:22 3.4	19:22 3.5	01:51 0.6	14:03 1.0	09:18 2.5	21:05 2.7	02:58 0.5	15:04 0.8	06:17 5.8	18:24 5.9
2 Wed		08:09 3.4	20:05 3.7	02:41 0.4	14:48 0.9	10:09 2.6	21:54 2.8	03:49 0.4	15:51 0.8	07:05 5.9	19:07 6.1
3 Thu		08:52 3.4	20:46 3.8	03:27 0.3	15:29 1.0	10:54 2.6	22:42 2.8	04:36 0.2	16:34 0.8	07:49 5.9	19:47 6.1
4 Fri		09:34 3.2	21:27 3.8	04:09 0.3	16:08 1.0	11:36 2.5	23:26 2.8	05:19 0.2	17:14 0.8	08:30 5.8	20:27 6.1
5 Sat		10:15 3.0	22:05 3.7	04:50 0.4	16:44 1.1		12:18 2.4	06:02 0.3	17:51 0.9	09:08 5.6	21:05 5.9
6 Sun		10:57 2.8	22:44 3.5	05:30 0.6	17:20 1.2	00:09 2.8	12:59 2.3	06:43 0.5	18:27 1.0	09:44 5.4	21:43 5.7
7 Mon		11:41 2.6	23:26 3.2	06:10 0.8	17:58 1.3	00:51 2.7	13:41 2.2	07:25 0.7	19:03 1.1	10:20 5.1	22:23 5.4
8 Tue	◐		12:30 2.5	06:53 1.0	18:44 1.4	01:35 2.5	14:27 2.1	08:09 0.9	19:45 1.2	11:00 4.9	23:08 5.1
9 Wed		00:17 3.0	13:33 2.4	07:44 1.2	19:45 1.5	02:22 2.4	15:20 2.1	08:57 1.1	20:42 1.3	11:50 4.6	
10 Thu		01:24 2.7	14:42 2.5	08:53 1.4	21:16 1.6	03:17 2.2	16:24 2.1	09:57 1.2	22:16 1.4	00:09 4.7	13:02 4.5
11 Fri		02:49 2.6	15:57 2.5	10:14 1.4	22:51 1.4	04:24 2.1	17:27 2.1	11:03 1.2	23:56 1.3	01:35 4.5	14:28 4.5
12 Sat		04:41 2.6	17:02 2.7	11:17 1.4	23:54 1.3	05:43 2.1	18:18 2.2		12:03 1.2	03:07 4.6	15:42 4.7
13 Sun		05:47 2.7	17:46 2.8		12:07 1.4	07:17 2.1	18:56 2.3	01:01 1.1	12:49 1.2	04:15 4.8	16:35 5.0
14 Mon		06:31 2.8	18:22 3.0	00:42 1.1	12:45 1.3	08:11 2.2	19:29 2.4	01:46 0.9	13:27 1.1	05:05 5.0	17:16 5.3
15 Tue		07:06 2.9	18:52 3.2	01:23 1.0	13:17 1.2	08:48 2.2	20:06 2.5	02:24 0.8	14:03 1.0	05:44 5.2	17:53 5.5
16 Wed	○	07:37 3.0	19:25 3.3	01:59 0.8	13:48 1.1	09:18 2.3	20:48 2.5	02:59 0.6	14:42 0.9	06:20 5.4	18:26 5.7
17 Thu		08:06 3.0	19:57 3.5	02:36 0.7	14:23 1.0	09:47 2.4	21:33 2.6	03:35 0.5	15:23 0.8	06:53 5.6	18:59 5.8
18 Fri		08:37 3.0	20:32 3.6	03:12 0.6	14:59 1.0	10:21 2.4	22:17 2.6	04:13 0.4	16:03 0.8	07:26 5.6	19:32 5.9
19 Sat		09:08 3.0	21:06 3.6	03:49 0.6	15:34 0.9	10:58 2.4	22:57 2.6	04:51 0.4	16:41 0.8	07:59 5.7	20:05 6.0
20 Sun		09:41 3.0	21:39 3.6	04:25 0.6	16:08 1.0	11:34 2.3	23:35 2.6	05:30 0.4	17:16 0.8	08:33 5.7	20:38 5.9
21 Mon		10:15 2.9	22:15 3.5	05:01 0.6	16:43 1.0		12:10 2.3	06:08 0.5	17:51 0.8	09:08 5.6	21:14 5.8
22 Tue		10:56 2.8	22:56 3.4	05:38 0.7	17:23 1.1	00:09 2.6	12:47 2.2	06:47 0.6	18:25 0.9	09:45 5.4	21:53 5.7
23 Wed	●	11:43 2.7		06:20 0.8	18:13 1.2	00:45 2.5	13:28 2.1	07:30 0.8	19:07 1.0	10:26 5.2	22:40 5.4
24 Thu			12:43 2.6	07:13 1.0	19:17 1.3	01:30 2.5	14:24 2.1	08:24 0.9	20:10 1.1	11:20 5.0	23:44 5.1
25 Fri		01:01 3.0	14:00 2.6	08:25 1.2	20:48 1.3	02:37 2.4	15:48 2.1	09:35 1.1	22:04 1.1		12:32 4.8
26 Sat		02:29 2.9	15:15 2.6	09:50 1.2	22:23 1.2	04:30 2.4	17:10 2.2	10:52 1.1	23:33 1.0	01:15 4.9	14:05 4.8
27 Sun		04:00 3.0	16:25 2.8	11:04 1.2	23:45 1.0	06:04 2.3	18:09 2.2		12:02 1.1	03:01 5.0	15:34 5.0
28 Mon		05:33 3.1	17:30 3.0		12:11 1.2	07:27 2.3	19:01 2.4	00:51 0.8	13:09 1.1	04:24 5.2	16:38 5.4

Tidal information computed by POLTIPS software developed by National Oceanography Centre

March 2022

Times: GMT / BST

Heights: metres (above chart datum)

Day	HUNSTANTON HW AM	LW AM	HW PM	LW PM	CROMER/SHERINGHAM HW AM	LW AM	HW PM	LW PM	BLAKENEY BAR HW AM	HW PM
1 Tue	05:33 6.5		17:37 6.6	12:09 1.3	05:40 4.7		17:43 5.0	12:08 1.2	05:30 5.2	17:35 5.4
2 Wed ●	06:22 6.8	00:54 0.6	18:21 7.0	13:01 1.0	06:26 4.8	00:57 0.7	18:25 5.0	12:55 1.0	06:18 5.5	18:17 5.6
3 Thu	07:05 7.2	01:44 0.3	19:00 7.2	13:45 0.9	07:07 4.9	01:48 0.5	19:04 5.2	13:37 0.9	06:58 5.6	18:55 5.8
4 Fri	07:42 7.1	02:26 0.2	19:35 7.2	14:21 0.8	07:44 4.9	02:32 0.4	19:41 5.2	14:15 0.8	07:35 5.6	19:32 5.9
5 Sat	08:16 7.0	03:02 0.2	20:09 7.2	14:52 0.8	08:18 4.8	03:08 0.4	20:15 5.2	14:49 0.8	08:09 5.5	20:08 5.8
6 Sun	08:48 6.8	03:33 0.5	20:42 7.0	15:19 0.9	08:51 4.7	03:37 0.6	20:51 5.1	15:21 0.9	08:42 5.4	20:44 5.7
7 Mon	09:18 6.5	03:58 0.8	21:17 6.7	15:45 1.1	09:23 4.6	04:00 0.8	21:26 4.8	15:51 1.1	09:13 5.2	21:19 5.4
8 Tue	09:49 6.1	04:20 1.2	21:54 6.2	16:13 1.4	09:56 4.4	04:21 1.1	22:04 4.5	16:22 1.3	09:44 5.0	21:56 5.1
9 Wed	10:24 5.7	04:45 1.6	22:37 5.7	16:48 1.8	10:33 4.1	04:48 1.4	22:49 4.2	16:58 1.6	10:17 4.7	22:36 4.7
10 Thu ◑	11:07 5.3	05:17 2.1	23:34 5.2	17:32 2.2	11:20 3.8	05:25 1.8	23:56 3.8	17:47 1.9	11:00 4.4	23:31 4.3
11 Fri		06:03 2.5	12:11 4.9	18:36 2.6		06:19 2.1	12:35 3.6	19:03 2.1		12:01 4.2
12 Sat	01:06 4.8	07:15 2.8	13:49 4.8	20:10 2.7	01:46 3.6	07:47 2.3	14:17 3.6	20:50 2.1	00:59 4.1	13:38 4.0
13 Sun	02:51 4.9	08:47 2.7	15:14 5.0	21:42 2.4	03:15 3.6	09:31 2.3	15:33 3.8	22:15 1.9	02:46 4.1	15:12 4.2
14 Mon	04:02 5.2	10:00 2.4	16:10 5.5	22:48 2.0	04:18 3.8	10:37 2.0	16:27 4.0	23:10 1.6	04:01 4.4	16:14 4.5
15 Tue	04:53 5.7	10:57 1.9	16:53 5.9	23:44 1.5	05:02 4.1	11:23 1.7	17:08 4.3	23:55 1.3	04:49 4.7	16:57 4.9
16 Wed	05:35 6.1	11:47 1.6	17:30 6.3		05:36 4.4		17:42 4.6	12:03 1.4	05:28 5.0	17:33 5.2
17 Thu	06:12 6.5	00:34 1.1	18:03 6.7	12:34 1.2	06:09 4.6	00:36 1.0	18:13 4.6	12:40 1.2	06:01 5.2	18:06 5.4
18 Fri ○	06:46 6.8	01:19 0.8	18:36 7.0	13:18 1.0	06:42 4.8	01:15 0.8	18:44 5.0	13:16 1.0	06:34 5.4	18:38 5.6
19 Sat	07:18 6.9	02:00 0.6	19:08 7.2	13:58 0.8	07:16 4.9	01:52 0.6	19:16 5.1	13:51 0.8	07:07 5.5	19:12 5.7
20 Sun	07:48 6.9	02:37 0.5	19:42 7.2	14:36 0.8	07:51 4.9	02:27 0.5	19:51 5.2	14:25 0.8	07:40 5.6	19:46 5.8
21 Mon	08:19 6.8	03:11 0.5	20:17 7.2	15:09 0.8	08:27 4.9	02:59 0.5	20:27 5.2	14:57 0.9	08:14 5.5	20:23 5.8
22 Tue	08:52 6.7	03:43 0.7	20:57 7.0	15:42 1.0	09:03 4.8	03:29 0.6	21:08 5.0	15:31 0.9	08:50 5.4	21:01 5.6
23 Wed	09:30 6.4	04:14 0.9	21:44 6.6	16:17 1.2	09:42 4.6	04:02 0.8	21:55 4.8	16:09 1.0	09:28 5.2	21:44 5.4
24 Thu	10:15 6.0	04:48 1.3	22:43 6.0	16:58 1.6	10:27 4.4	04:41 1.1	22:54 4.4	16:56 1.3	10:12 5.0	22:39 5.2
25 Fri ●	11:15 5.6	05:32 1.8		17:57 1.9	11:25 4.1	05:33 1.5		18:00 1.5	11:08 4.7	23:54 4.6
26 Sat	00:05 5.5	06:36 2.2	12:40 5.3	19:24 2.0	00:18 4.1	06:47 1.9	12:49 3.9	19:31 1.7		12:26 4.4
27 Sun	02:51 5.3	09:12 2.4	15:18 5.4	22:14 1.8	03:09 4.0	09:31 2.0	15:28 3.9	22:24 1.5	02:43 4.4	15:09 4.4
28 Mon	04:24 5.6	10:48 2.2	16:34 5.7	23:39 1.4	04:39 4.1	11:01 1.8	16:44 4.2	23:47 1.2	04:24 4.6	16:35 4.7
29 Tue	05:29 6.0		17:32 6.2	12:00 1.8	05:43 4.4		17:34 4.5	12:03 1.2	05:32 5.0	17:34 5.1
30 Wed	06:21 6.5	00:44 0.9	18:19 6.6	12:55 1.4	06:30 4.6	00:51 0.9	18:26 4.8	12:51 1.3	06:22 5.3	18:19 5.4

Tidal information computed by POLTIPS software developed by National Oceanography Centre

March 2022

Times: GMT / BST

Heights: metres (above chart datum)

Day		WINTERTON HW AM	HW PM	LW AM	LW PM	GORLESTON HW AM	HW PM	LW AM	LW PM	WELLS BAR HW AM	HW PM
1 Tue		06:31 3.2	18:21 3.3	00:51 0.7	13:07 1.1	08:30 2.4	19:51 2.5	01:57 0.6	14:09 1.0	05:23 5.6	17:28 5.7
2 Wed ●		07:15 3.3	19:04 3.5	01:43 0.5	13:52 1.0	09:15 2.5	21:04 2.5	02:48 0.4	14:54 0.9	06:12 5.8	18:11 5.9
3 Thu		07:54 3.3	19:45 3.7	02:27 0.3	14:32 0.9	09:54 2.5	21:34 2.7	03:33 0.2	15:35 0.8	06:53 5.9	18:50 6.1
4 Fri		08:32 3.2	20:25 3.8	03:08 0.3	15:08 0.9	10:33 2.5	22:20 2.8	04:15 0.2	16:14 0.7	07:30 5.9	19:27 6.2
5 Sat		09:09 3.1	21:04 3.7	03:46 0.3	15:43 0.9	11:10 2.5	23:03 2.8	04:54 0.2	16:51 0.7	08:04 5.8	20:03 6.1
6 Sun		09:44 3.0	21:40 3.6	04:22 0.4	16:15 0.9	11:47 2.4	23:44 2.7	05:33 0.3	17:26 0.8	08:36 5.7	20:38 6.0
7 Mon		10:18 2.8	22:16 3.4	04:56 0.6	16:48 1.0		12:24 2.3	06:11 0.5	17:57 0.9	09:06 5.5	21:12 5.7
8 Tue		10:53 2.7	22:56 3.1	05:30 0.8	17:23 1.1	00:22 2.6	12:59 2.2	06:46 0.7	18:24 1.0	09:36 5.3	21:47 5.4
9 Wed		11:31 2.6	23:45 2.8	06:05 1.1	18:05 1.3	01:00 2.4	13:35 2.2	07:18 1.0	18:57 1.1	10:08 5.0	22:26 5.0
10 Thu ◐				06:47 1.3	18:59 1.4	01:42 2.2	14:17 2.1	07:51 1.2	19:48 1.2	10:49 4.7	23:19 4.6
11 Fri		00:52 2.6	13:25 2.4	07:45 1.5	20:18 1.5	02:33 2.1	15:12 2.1	08:31 1.3	21:09 1.3	11:48 4.5	
12 Sat		02:22 2.4	14:42 2.4	09:30 1.6	22:22 1.4	03:42 2.0	16:15 2.1	09:42 1.4	23:23 1.2	00:44 4.4	13:23 4.3
13 Sun		04:19 2.5	16:00 2.5	10:58 1.6	23:28 1.2	05:16 2.0	17:15 2.1	11:15 1.4		02:32 4.4	14:59 4.5
14 Mon		05:27 2.6	17:05 2.7	11:47 1.5		07:08 2.1	18:08 2.2	00:26 1.0	12:17 1.3	03:50 4.6	16:03 4.8
15 Tue		06:08 2.8	17:47 2.9	00:15 1.1	12:23 1.4	07:51 2.2	18:57 2.3	01:10 0.8	13:04 1.2	04:40 5.0	16:48 5.2
16 Wed		06:40 2.9	18:22 3.1	00:55 0.9	12:55 1.2	08:27 2.3	19:43 2.4	01:50 0.6	13:47 1.1	05:20 5.2	17:26 5.5
17 Thu		07:10 3.0	18:56 3.3	01:32 0.7	13:28 1.0	08:53 2.4	20:30 2.5	02:29 0.5	14:28 0.8	05:55 5.5	18:00 5.5
18 Fri ○		07:38 3.1	19:31 3.5	02:08 0.6	14:03 0.9	09:27 2.4	21:15 2.6	03:09 0.3	15:09 0.7	06:28 5.6	18:33 5.9
19 Sat		08:09 3.2	20:06 3.6	02:45 0.5	14:40 0.8	10:03 2.4	21:58 2.6	03:49 0.3	15:48 0.7	07:02 5.8	19:07 6.0
20 Sun		08:41 3.2	20:42 3.7	03:22 0.4	15:17 0.8	10:38 2.4	22:38 2.7	04:27 0.2	16:24 0.6	07:35 5.8	19:41 6.1
21 Mon		09:14 3.1	21:18 3.6	03:58 0.4	15:52 0.8	11:12 2.4	23:14 2.7	05:05 0.3	16:57 0.7	08:09 5.8	20:17 6.1
22 Tue		09:50 3.0	21:57 3.5	04:34 0.6	16:28 0.9	11:45 2.3	23:50 2.6	05:41 0.4	17:30 0.7	08:44 5.7	20:54 5.9
23 Wed		10:28 2.9	22:42 3.4	05:11 0.7	16:59 1.0		12:18 2.2	06:16 0.6	18:06 0.8	09:20 5.5	21:36 5.5
24 Thu		11:13 2.8	23:42 3.1	05:53 0.9	18:02 1.0	00:32 2.5	12:57 2.2	06:55 0.8	18:53 0.9	10:03 5.3	22:29 5.3
25 Fri ●			12:12 2.6	06:49 1.2	19:11 1.1	01:28 2.4	13:53 2.2	07:49 1.1	20:18 1.0	10:56 5.0	23:41 4.9
26 Sat		01:03 2.9	13:27 2.5	08:07 1.4	20:47 1.1	02:48 2.2	15:08 2.1	09:05 1.2	21:58 1.0		12:12 4.7
27 Sun		03:42 2.8	15:48 2.6	10:43 1.4	23:24 1.0	05:45 2.2	17:31 2.2	11:30 1.3		02:28 4.8	14:54 4.7
28 Mon		05:27 2.9	17:06 2.7		12:01 1.4	07:23 2.3	18:38 2.2	00:28 0.8	12:51 1.3	04:11 5.0	16:23 5.0
29 Tue		06:35 3.1	18:11 3.0	00:40 0.8	13:03 1.3	08:32 2.4	19:34 2.4	01:44 0.6	14:06 1.2	05:22 5.3	17:24 5.4
30 Wed		07:21 3.2	19:01 3.2	01:38 0.6	13:52 1.2	09:18 2.4	20:28 2.5	02:42 0.4	14:56 1.0	06:14 5.6	18:11 5.7
31 Thu		07:58 3.2	19:43 3.4	02:25 0.4	14:32 1.0	09:57 2.5	21:21 2.6	03:28 0.3	15:35 0.8	06:56 5.7	18:50 5.9

Tidal information computed by POLTIPS software developed by National Oceanography Centre

Times: GMT / BST

April 2022

Heights: metres (above chart datum)

Day			HUNSTANTON HW AM		HW PM		LW AM		LW PM		CROMER/SHERINGHAM HW AM		HW PM		LW AM		LW PM		BLAKENEY BAR HW AM		HW PM	
1	Fri	●	07:41	7.0	19:36	7.1	02:21	0.3	14:20	0.9	07:45	4.8	19:42	5.1	02:27	0.5	14:13	0.9	07:37	5.5	19:32	5.7
2	Sat		08:15	7.0	20:09	7.2	02:59	0.3	14:54	0.8	08:17	4.9	20:17	5.2	03:03	0.5	14:50	0.8	08:08	5.5	20:07	5.8
3	Sun		08:45	6.9	20:42	7.0	03:30	0.5	15:23	0.8	08:48	4.8	20:51	5.1	03:33	0.6	15:23	0.8	08:39	5.5	20:43	5.7
4	Mon		09:13	6.8	21:13	6.8	03:57	0.8	15:49	0.9	09:18	4.8	21:24	4.9	03:56	0.7	15:54	0.9	09:09	5.4	21:18	5.6
5	Tue		09:41	6.5	21:46	6.5	04:17	1.0	16:14	1.1	09:47	4.6	21:59	4.7	04:16	0.9	16:22	1.0	09:38	5.2	21:51	5.3
6	Wed		10:09	6.2	22:21	6.1	04:37	1.4	16:42	1.4	10:17	4.5	22:36	4.4	04:39	1.2	16:52	1.2	10:08	5.1	22:25	5.0
7	Thu		10:38	5.8	23:01	5.6	05:01	1.7	17:14	1.8	10:49	4.2	23:18	4.1	05:07	1.4	17:27	1.5	10:38	4.8	23:05	4.6
8	Fri		11:13	5.4	23:55	5.1	05:33	2.0	17:54	2.1	11:29	4.0			05:42	1.8	18:11	1.8	11:16	4.6	23:56	4.3
9	Sat	◐			12:05	5.0	06:15	2.5	18:51	2.4	00:19	3.7	12:30	3.7	06:30	2.1	19:20	2.0			12:11	4.3
10	Sun		01:22	4.8	13:36	4.8	07:19	2.8	20:18	2.6	02:00	3.5	14:18	3.6	07:48	2.4	20:59	2.0	01:16	4.0	13:37	4.1
11	Mon		03:10	4.8	15:18	4.9	08:53	2.8	22:00	2.3	03:35	3.6	15:45	3.7	09:34	2.4	22:29	1.8	03:00	4.0	15:18	4.2
12	Tue		04:26	5.2	16:24	5.4	10:21	2.5	23:14	1.9	04:39	3.8	16:45	4.0	10:55	2.1	23:30	1.5	04:18	4.3	16:29	4.4
13	Wed		05:18	5.6	17:11	5.8	11:24	2.1			05:26	4.1	17:28	4.2	11:47	1.8			05:12	4.6	17:18	4.8
14	Thu		06:00	6.1	17:51	6.3	00:12	1.4	12:17	1.6	06:03	4.3	18:03	4.5	00:17	1.2	12:30	1.4	05:53	4.9	17:58	5.1
15	Fri		06:37	6.5	18:28	6.7	01:02	1.1	13:05	1.2	06:36	4.6	18:37	4.8	01:00	0.9	13:09	1.2	06:29	5.2	18:33	5.4
16	Sat	○	07:12	6.8	19:03	7.0	01:48	0.8	13:51	1.0	07:11	4.8	19:12	5.0	01:42	0.7	13:48	1.0	07:04	5.4	19:08	5.6
17	Sun		07:45	6.9	19:40	7.2	02:29	0.6	14:33	0.8	07:47	4.9	19:49	5.1	02:21	0.6	14:25	0.8	07:38	5.5	19:44	5.8
18	Mon		08:17	7.0	20:18	7.3	03:08	0.5	15:12	0.7	08:24	5.0	20:30	5.2	02:57	0.5	15:03	0.7	08:13	5.6	20:23	5.8
19	Tue		08:51	6.9	21:00	7.2	03:44	0.5	15:50	0.8	09:02	5.0	21:13	5.1	03:33	0.5	15:39	0.7	08:50	5.6	21:04	5.8
20	Wed		09:28	6.8	21:46	6.8	04:18	0.7	16:28	0.9	09:40	4.9	22:01	5.0	04:08	0.7	16:18	0.8	09:29	5.5	21:48	5.6
21	Thu		10:09	6.5	22:40	6.4	04:53	1.0	17:09	1.1	10:22	4.7	22:56	4.7	04:45	0.9	17:00	0.9	10:10	5.3	22:40	5.3
22	Fri		10:59	6.1	23:48	5.8	05:31	1.4	17:56	1.4	11:10	4.4			05:29	1.3	17:54	1.2	10:59	5.0	23:43	4.9
23	Sat	◑			12:02	5.6	06:18	1.9	19:00	1.6	00:03	4.3	12:12	4.2	06:24	1.7	19:06	1.4	11:58	4.8		
24	Sun		01:14	5.4	13:26	5.4	07:24	2.3	20:30	1.7	01:33	4.0	13:40	4.0	07:42	2.0	20:46	1.5	01:08	4.6	13:17	4.5
25	Mon		02:49	5.4	14:57	5.5	09:00	2.5	22:05	1.5	03:10	4.0	15:11	4.1	09:19	2.1	22:21	1.3	02:53	4.5	14:55	4.6
26	Tue		04:08	5.6	16:09	5.8	10:30	2.2	23:19	1.1	04:29	4.2	16:21	4.3	10:39	1.9	23:31	1.1	04:13	4.8	16:14	4.8
27	Wed		05:08	6.0	17:06	6.2	11:35	1.8			05:27	4.4	17:16	4.5	11:37	1.6			05:14	5.0	17:10	5.1
28	Thu		05:55	6.4	17:52	6.5	00:18	0.8	12:26	1.5	06:09	4.5	18:00	4.7	00:27	0.9	12:24	1.4	06:00	5.2	17:54	5.3
29	Fri		06:36	6.6	18:32	6.8	01:06	0.7	13:09	1.2	06:45	4.6	18:39	4.9	01:13	0.8	13:07	1.1	06:37	5.3	18:31	5.4
30	Sat	●	07:11	6.8	19:09	6.8	01:48	0.7	13:48	1.0	07:17	4.7	19:17	4.9	01:52	0.7	13:46	1.0	07:09	5.4	19:08	5.5

Tidal information computed by POLTIPS software developed by National Oceanography Centre

April 2022

Times: GMT / BST

Date		Moon	WINTERTON HW AM	WINTERTON HW PM	WINTERTON LW AM	WINTERTON LW PM	GORLESTON HW AM	GORLESTON HW PM	GORLESTON LW AM	GORLESTON LW PM	WELLS BAR HW AM	WELLS BAR HW PM
1	Fri	●	08:34 3.2	20:24 3.6	03:05 0.4	15:09 0.9	10:31 2.5	22:12 2.6	04:09 0.2	16:13 0.7	07:32 5.8	19:26 6.0
2	Sat		09:08 3.2	21:03 3.6	03:43 0.4	15:44 0.8	11:06 2.5	22:57 2.7	04:49 0.2	16:51 0.6	08:03 5.8	20:02 6.1
3	Sun		09:41 3.1	21:41 3.5	04:17 0.4	16:17 0.8	11:42 2.4	23:39 2.6	05:27 0.3	17:27 0.6	08:34 5.8	20:38 6.0
4	Mon		10:12 3.0	22:16 3.4	04:50 0.6	16:50 0.9	12:16 2.4		06:03 0.5	18:01 0.7	09:04 5.7	21:12 5.9
5	Tue		10:43 2.9	22:52 3.2	05:21 0.8	17:22 0.9	00:18 2.5	12:48 2.3	06:36 0.7	18:28 0.8	09:32 5.6	21:45 5.6
6	Wed		11:13 2.8	23:33 2.9	05:50 1.0	17:56 1.0	00:53 2.4	13:13 2.3	07:00 0.9	18:50 0.9	10:01 5.4	22:18 5.3
7	Thu		11:47 2.8		06:20 1.2	18:36 1.1	01:22 2.3	13:30 2.2	07:13 1.0	19:21 1.0	10:30 5.1	22:56 5.0
8	Fri		00:22 2.7	12:30 2.6	06:56 1.4	19:27 1.2	01:57 2.1	14:05 2.2	07:36 1.2	20:09 1.1	11:07 4.9	23:45 4.6
9	Sat	◐	01:27 2.5	13:27 2.5	07:47 1.6	20:36 1.3	02:48 2.0	15:06 2.1	08:23 1.3	21:18 1.1	11:59 4.6	
10	Sun		02:55 2.4	14:42 2.4	09:10 1.7	22:24 1.3	03:59 1.9	16:18 2.1	09:30 1.4	23:12 1.1	01:02 4.3	13:23 4.4
11	Mon		04:27 2.5	16:00 2.5	11:19 1.7	23:42 1.1	05:28 1.9	17:28 2.1	11:05 1.4		02:45 4.3	15:03 4.4
12	Tue		05:44 2.6	17:07 2.6		12:07 1.5	07:10 2.0	18:30 2.2	00:30 0.9	12:33 1.3	04:05 4.6	16:16 4.8
13	Wed		06:30 2.8	17:59 2.8	00:32 1.0	12:43 1.4	07:59 2.2	19:25 2.2	01:21 0.8	13:29 1.1	05:01 4.9	17:07 5.1
14	Thu		07:04 2.9	18:42 3.0	01:14 0.8	13:18 1.2	08:37 2.3	20:15 2.3	02:07 0.6	14:17 1.0	05:44 5.2	17:49 5.4
15	Fri		07:34 3.0	19:21 3.2	01:54 0.7	13:56 1.0	09:15 2.4	21:04 2.4	02:53 0.4	15:01 0.8	06:22 5.5	18:26 5.7
16	Sat	○	08:05 3.1	20:00 3.5	02:34 0.5	14:36 0.9	09:55 2.4	21:50 2.5	03:36 0.3	15:44 0.7	06:58 5.7	19:02 5.9
17	Sun		08:37 3.2	20:39 3.6	03:13 0.4	15:17 0.8	10:34 2.4	22:33 2.6	04:19 0.2	16:24 0.6	07:33 5.8	19:39 6.1
18	Mon		09:13 3.3	21:18 3.7	03:53 0.4	15:57 0.7	11:12 2.4	23:15 2.6	05:00 0.2	17:03 0.6	08:08 5.9	20:18 6.1
19	Tue		09:49 3.3	22:01 3.6	04:31 0.5	16:38 0.7	11:48 2.4	23:56 2.6	05:38 0.4	17:40 0.6	08:45 5.9	20:59 6.1
20	Wed		10:27 3.2	22:47 3.5	05:10 0.6	17:20 0.8		12:21 2.4	06:15 0.5	18:18 0.6	09:23 5.8	21:42 5.9
21	Thu		11:08 3.0	23:40 3.2	05:50 0.8	18:08 0.8	00:39 2.6	12:57 2.3	06:51 0.7	19:04 0.7	10:03 5.6	22:32 5.6
22	Fri		11:56 2.9		06:37 1.1	19:05 0.9	01:32 2.4	13:42 2.3	07:34 1.0	20:10 0.7	10:50 5.3	23:32 5.2
23	Sat	◑	00:47 3.0	12:53 2.8	07:35 1.3	20:17 0.9	02:39 2.3	14:42 2.3	08:34 1.2	21:29 0.8	11:47 5.0	
24	Sun		02:13 2.8	14:03 2.7	08:56 1.5	21:47 0.9	04:06 2.2	15:53 2.2	09:48 1.3	22:51 0.7	00:54 4.9	13:03 4.8
25	Mon		03:54 2.9	15:20 2.7	10:28 1.5	23:10 0.8	05:47 2.2	17:05 2.2	11:07 1.4		02:38 4.8	14:40 4.9
26	Tue		05:19 3.0	16:38 2.8	11:41 1.5		07:08 2.3	18:12 2.3	00:10 0.8	12:25 1.3	04:00 5.0	16:01 5.1
27	Wed		06:18 3.0	17:47 3.0	00:19 1.7	12:39 1.3	08:08 2.3	19:11 2.4	01:18 0.5	13:36 1.2	05:03 5.3	16:59 5.4
28	Thu		07:01 3.1	18:37 3.2	01:14 0.6	13:26 1.2	08:53 2.4	20:06 2.4	02:15 0.4	14:27 1.0	05:51 5.5	17:45 5.6
29	Fri		07:37 3.1	19:21 3.3	01:59 0.5	14:07 1.1	09:30 2.4	21:00 2.5	03:00 0.4	15:09 0.8	06:30 5.6	18:24 5.8
30	Sat	●	08:10 3.1	20:02 3.4	02:38 0.5	14:44 0.9	10:04 2.4	21:50 2.5	03:42 0.4	15:49 0.7	07:03 5.6	19:02 5.8

Tidal information computed by POLTIPS software developed by National Oceanography Centre

May 2022

Times: GMT / BST

Heights: metres (above chart datum)

		HUNSTANTON				CROMER/SHERINGHAM				BLAKENEY BAR	
		HW AM	HW PM	LW AM	LW PM	HW AM	HW PM	LW AM	LW PM	HW AM	HW PM
1 Sun		07:42 6.8	19:42 6.8	02:23 0.8	14:21 1.0	07:47 4.8	19:53 4.9	02:24 0.8	14:24 0.9	07:38 5.4	19:43 5.6
2 Mon		08:12 6.8	20:15 6.7	02:51 0.9	14:51 1.0	08:18 4.8	20:29 4.8	02:51 0.8	14:58 0.9	08:09 5.4	20:19 5.5
3 Tue		08:39 6.6	20:48 6.5	03:14 1.1	15:18 1.1	08:48 4.7	21:05 4.7	03:16 0.9	15:30 1.0	08:40 5.4	20:55 5.4
4 Wed		09:06 6.5	21:22 6.3	03:35 1.3	15:46 1.2	09:18 4.6	21:40 4.5	03:42 1.1	16:00 1.1	09:09 5.3	21:30 5.1
5 Thu		09:33 6.2	21:58 6.0	03:58 1.5	16:15 1.4	09:47 4.5	22:18 4.3	04:09 1.2	16:31 1.2	09:39 5.1	22:06 4.9
6 Fri		10:03 5.9	22:41 5.6	04:26 1.7	16:48 1.7	10:18 4.4	23:02 4.0	04:39 1.5	17:06 1.4	10:11 4.9	22:44 4.6
7 Sat		10:37 5.6	23:35 5.2	05:00 2.0	17:28 1.9	10:57 4.1	23:57 3.8	05:16 1.7	17:51 1.6	10:49 4.7	23:34 4.4
8 Sun	●	11:25 5.3		05:42 2.3	18:21 2.1	11:51 3.9		06:01 2.0	18:52 1.8	11:39 4.4	
9 Mon		00:48 4.9	12:38 5.0	06:39 2.6	19:33 2.3	01:12 3.6	13:15 3.8	07:05 2.2	20:13 1.8	00:42 4.2	12:50 4.3
10 Tue		02:16 4.9	14:09 5.1	07:57 2.8	21:03 2.2	02:36 3.6	14:42 3.8	08:31 2.3	21:33 1.7	02:08 4.2	14:17 4.3
11 Wed		03:32 5.2	15:23 5.4	09:25 2.6	22:21 1.8	03:45 3.8	15:46 4.0	09:54 2.1	22:38 1.5	03:23 4.3	15:31 4.5
12 Thu		04:28 5.6	16:18 5.8	10:36 2.2	23:22 1.5	04:38 4.0	16:35 4.2	10:57 1.8	23:31 1.2	04:21 4.6	16:27 4.8
13 Fri		05:14 6.3	17:05 6.3	11:33 1.8		05:21 4.3	17:17 4.5	11:48 1.5		05:10 4.9	17:13 5.1
14 Sat		05:54 6.4	17:48 6.7	00:16 1.2	12:25 1.4	06:00 4.6	17:58 4.8	00:18 0.9	12:33 1.3	05:52 5.2	17:56 5.4
15 Sun		06:32 6.7	18:31 7.0	01:06 0.9	13:15 1.2	06:39 4.8	18:41 5.0	01:03 0.7	13:15 1.0	06:31 5.4	18:37 5.6
16 Mon	○	07:10 6.9	19:15 7.1	01:52 0.7	14:03 1.0	07:18 4.9	19:27 5.1	01:47 0.6	13:59 0.8	07:10 5.5	19:20 5.7
17 Tue		07:48 7.0	20:01 7.1	02:35 0.6	14:49 0.8	07:58 5.0	20:15 5.1	02:29 0.6	14:42 0.7	07:49 5.6	20:05 5.8
18 Wed		08:28 6.9	20:51 7.0	03:16 0.6	15:33 0.8	08:40 5.0	21:07 5.0	03:11 0.6	15:27 0.6	08:31 5.6	20:54 5.7
19 Thu		09:11 6.8	21:45 6.7	03:56 0.8	16:18 0.8	09:23 4.9	22:01 4.9	03:52 0.8	16:13 0.7	09:13 5.5	21:46 5.5
20 Fri		09:57 6.5	22:45 6.3	04:36 1.1	17:06 0.9	10:09 4.8	23:00 4.6	04:36 1.1	17:05 0.8	10:01 5.4	22:43 5.2
21 Sat		10:48 6.2	23:51 5.9	05:18 1.5	17:59 1.1	11:01 4.6		05:24 1.4	18:06 1.0	10:52 5.2	23:50 4.9
22 Sun	◐	11:48 5.9		06:07 1.9	19:03 1.2	00:09 4.3	12:04 4.4	06:20 1.7	19:21 1.2	11:51 5.0	
23 Mon		01:06 5.6	13:03 5.6	07:09 2.3	20:18 1.4	01:29 4.1	13:22 4.3	07:29 1.9	20:41 1.2	01:14 4.7	13:03 4.8
24 Tue		02:24 5.5	14:22 5.6	08:29 2.4	21:35 1.3	02:49 4.1	14:41 4.3	08:48 2.0	21:55 1.2	02:35 4.7	14:26 4.9
25 Wed		03:34 5.6	15:33 5.8	09:49 2.2	22:42 1.2	04:00 4.1	15:48 4.5	10:01 1.9	22:57 1.1	03:44 4.8	15:39 4.9
26 Thu		04:32 5.8	16:31 6.0	10:54 2.0	23:39 1.1	04:55 4.2	16:43 4.5	11:01 1.7	23:50 1.0	04:41 4.9	16:38 5.0
27 Fri		05:21 6.1	17:20 6.3	11:47 1.7		05:39 4.3	17:31 4.6	11:51 1.5		05:28 5.0	17:24 5.1
28 Sat		06:02 6.3	18:03 6.4	00:26 1.1	12:32 1.4	06:15 4.5	18:14 4.6	00:34 1.0	12:37 1.3	06:06 5.1	18:06 5.2
29 Sun		06:39 6.5	18:43 6.4	01:06 1.2	13:12 1.3	06:48 4.6	18:54 4.7	01:12 1.0	13:20 1.2	06:39 5.2	18:45 5.3
30 Mon	●	07:12 6.6	19:20 6.4	01:39 1.2	13:48 1.3	07:20 4.6	19:34 4.7	01:45 1.0	14:00 1.1	07:11 5.2	19:23 5.3

Tidal information computed by POLTIPS software developed by National Oceanography Centre

May 2022

Times: GMT / BST

Heights: metres (above chart datum)

Day		WINTERTON HW AM	WINTERTON HW PM	WINTERTON LW AM	WINTERTON LW PM	GORLESTON HW AM	GORLESTON HW PM	GORLESTON LW AM	GORLESTON LW PM	WELLS BAR HW AM	WELLS BAR HW PM
1 Sun		08:42 3.2	20:42 3.4	03:14 0.6	15:20 0.8	10:39 2.4	22:36 2.5	04:21 0.4	16:28 0.6	07:33 5.7	19:38 5.9
2 Mon		09:14 3.2	21:20 3.3	03:47 0.7	15:55 0.8	11:13 2.4	23:16 2.4	04:57 0.5	17:05 0.7	08:04 5.7	20:14 5.8
3 Tue		09:44 3.1	21:58 3.1	04:18 0.8	16:29 0.8	11:44 2.4	23:51 2.4	05:30 0.7	17:37 0.7	08:35 5.7	20:50 5.6
4 Wed		10:11 3.1	22:35 2.9	04:46 1.0	17:02 0.9	12:05 2.4		05:53 0.8	18:00 0.8	09:04 5.6	21:24 5.4
5 Thu		10:39 3.0	23:15 2.8	05:11 1.1	17:37 1.0	00:17 2.3	12:08 2.4	06:01 0.9	18:24 0.8	09:33 5.4	21:59 5.2
6 Fri		11:12 2.9		05:37 1.2	18:17 1.0	00:41 2.2	12:39 2.4	06:24 1.0	18:59 0.9	10:04 5.2	22:36 4.9
7 Sat		00:05 2.6	*11:53 2.8	06:12 1.4	19:05 1.1	01:20 2.1	13:25 2.3	07:02 1.1	19:48 0.9	10:41 5.0	23:24 4.7
8 Sun		01:03 2.5	12:45 2.7	07:02 1.6	20:06 1.2	02:13 2.0	14:24 2.2	07:51 1.3	20:54 1.0	11:29 4.8	
9 Mon ◐		02:18 2.4	13:47 2.6	07:51 1.7	21:21 1.2	03:22 2.0	15:37 2.2	08:57 1.4	22:14 1.0	00:29 4.5	12:37 4.6
10 Tue		03:34 2.5	15:01 2.6	09:44 1.7	22:35 1.1	04:42 2.0	16:49 2.1	10:19 1.4	23:34 0.8	01:53 4.4	14:02 4.6
11 Wed		04:39 2.6	16:12 2.6	10:58 1.6	23:33 0.9	06:01 2.0	17:55 2.2	11:44 1.3		03:08 4.6	15:17 4.8
12 Thu		05:33 2.8	17:08 2.8	11:50 1.4		07:03 2.2	18:54 2.2	00:35 0.7	12:48 1.1	04:09 4.9	16:14 5.1
13 Fri		06:16 2.9	17:58 3.0	00:23 0.8	12:36 1.3	07:53 2.2	19:45 2.3	01:27 0.5	13:42 1.0	04:59 5.2	17:02 5.4
14 Sat		06:55 3.0	18:44 3.2	01:11 0.7	13:22 1.1	08:39 2.3	20:35 2.4	02:17 0.4	14:30 0.8	05:43 5.5	17:47 5.7
15 Sun		07:31 3.2	19:29 3.4	01:56 0.6	14:08 0.9	09:24 2.4	21:22 2.5	03:03 0.3	15:16 0.7	06:24 5.7	18:30 5.9
16 Mon ○		08:09 3.3	20:15 3.5	02:41 0.5	14:55 0.8	10:06 2.4	22:09 2.6	03:49 0.3	16:01 0.6	07:04 5.8	19:14 6.0
17 Tue		08:48 3.3	21:02 3.6	03:24 0.5	15:41 0.7	10:46 2.4	22:57 2.6	04:32 0.4	16:46 0.6	07:44 5.9	20:00 6.0
18 Wed		09:28 3.4	21:52 3.5	04:08 0.6	16:29 0.6	11:25 2.4	23:46 2.6	05:13 0.5	17:32 0.5	08:26 5.9	20:49 6.0
19 Thu		10:09 3.3	22:46 3.4	04:51 0.8	17:18 0.6		12:04 2.4	05:54 0.6	18:23 0.5	09:08 5.8	21:40 5.8
20 Fri		10:54 3.3	23:44 3.2	05:36 1.0	18:11 0.6	00:41 2.5	12:47 2.4	06:37 0.8	19:19 0.6	09:54 5.7	22:35 5.5
21 Sat		11:43 3.1		06:26 1.2	19:08 0.6	01:42 2.4	13:38 2.4	07:27 1.0	20:19 0.6	10:44 5.5	23:39 5.2
22 Sun ◑		00:50 3.0	12:38 3.0	07:24 1.4	20:14 0.7	02:48 2.3	14:36 2.4	08:26 1.2	21:24 0.6	11:40 5.2	
23 Mon		02:12 2.9	13:39 2.9	08:34 1.5	21:28 0.7	04:01 2.3	15:39 2.4	09:29 1.3	22:32 0.6	01:00 5.0	12:49 5.1
24 Tue		03:37 2.9	14:48 2.9	09:53 1.6	22:41 0.7	05:21 2.2	16:42 2.4	10:36 1.3	23:41 0.6	02:20 5.0	14:11 5.1
25 Wed		04:50 2.9	16:03 2.9	11:02 1.5	23:47 0.7	06:33 2.3	17:46 2.4	11:45 1.3		03:30 5.1	15:25 5.2
26 Thu		05:49 2.9	17:14 3.0		12:56 1.3	07:31 2.3	18:47 2.4	00:45 0.5	12:52 1.0	04:29 5.2	16:26 5.3
27 Fri		06:33 3.0	18:11 3.0	00:43 0.7	13:40 1.1	08:19 2.3	19:45 2.4	01:42 0.6	13:52 1.0	05:18 5.3	17:14 5.4
28 Sat		07:12 3.0	19:01 3.1	01:29 0.7	14:21 1.1	09:00 2.3	20:39 2.3	02:30 0.6	14:43 0.9	05:58 5.4	17:58 5.5
29 Sun		07:46 3.1	19:45 3.1	02:08 0.8	15:00 0.9	09:38 2.4	21:30 2.4	03:13 0.6	15:28 0.8	06:32 5.5	18:38 5.6
30 Mon ●		08:19 3.2	20:28 3.1	02:44 0.8	15:38 0.9	10:13 2.4	22:16 2.4	03:52 0.7	16:09 0.8	07:05 5.6	19:17 5.6
31 Tue		08:49 3.2	21:09 3.0	03:17 0.9		10:45 2.4	22:56 2.3	04:26 0.8	16:47 0.7	07:38 5.6	19:56 5.6

Tidal information computed by POLTIPS software developed by National Oceanography Centre

Times: GMT / BST — June 2022

Heights: metres (above chart datum)

Date	HUNSTANTON HW AM	HW PM	LW AM	LW PM	CROMER/SHERINGHAM HW AM	HW PM	LW AM	LW PM	BLAKENEY BAR HW AM	HW PM
1 Wed	08:12 6.5	20:32 6.2	02:33 1.3	14:53 1.3	08:24 4.7	20:51 4.5	02:46 1.1	15:12 1.0	08:16 5.3	20:37 5.2
2 Thu	08:40 6.4	21:09 6.1	03:00 1.4	15:24 1.4	08:56 4.7	21:28 4.4	03:16 1.2	15:45 1.1	08:48 5.2	21:13 5.0
3 Fri	09:09 6.2	21:47 5.9	03:29 1.5	15:57 1.4	09:27 4.6	22:06 4.3	03:48 1.3	16:18 1.2	09:20 5.2	21:50 4.9
4 Sat	09:39 6.1	22:31 5.5	04:02 1.7	16:33 1.5	10:00 4.5	22:48 4.1	04:21 1.5	16:55 1.3	09:54 5.0	22:31 4.7
5 Sun	10:15 5.9	23:18 5.5	04:38 1.9	17:12 1.7	10:37 4.3	23:36 4.0	04:59 1.6	17:38 1.4	10:34 4.9	23:15 4.6
6 Mon	11:00 5.7		05:19 2.1	18:00 1.8	11:24 4.2		05:41 1.8	18:30 1.5	11:19 4.7	
7 Tue ◐	00:15 5.2	*11:59 5.5	06:09 2.4	18:58 1.9	00:31 3.9	12:23 4.1	06:32 2.0	19:31 1.6	00:11 4.4	12:14 4.4
8 Wed	01:20 5.2	13:09 5.4	07:10 2.5	20:05 1.9	01:36 3.8	13:33 4.0	07:36 2.1	20:37 1.5	01:15 4.4	13:19 4.4
9 Thu	02:27 5.2	14:21 5.6	08:21 2.4	21:14 1.8	02:41 3.9	14:39 4.1	08:48 2.0	21:41 1.4	02:26 4.4	14:30 4.6
10 Fri	03:27 5.1	15:24 5.9	09:32 2.3	22:21 1.6	03:42 4.0	15:37 4.3	09:57 1.9	22:41 1.2	03:28 4.6	15:33 4.8
11 Sat	04:21 5.8	16:21 6.2	10:38 2.0	23:23 1.4	04:35 4.2	16:33 4.5	10:59 1.6	23:36 1.0	04:24 4.8	16:30 5.0
12 Sun	05:10 6.2	17:14 6.5	11:39 1.7		05:23 4.5	17:26 4.7	11:54 1.4		05:15 5.1	17:21 5.3
13 Mon	05:57 6.5	18:06 6.7	00:21 1.2	12:39 1.4	06:08 4.7	18:20 4.9	00:28 0.9	12:45 1.1	06:02 5.3	18:13 5.5
14 Tue ○	06:42 6.7	19:00 6.9	01:15 1.0	13:37 1.2	06:53 4.8	19:15 5.0	01:18 0.8	13:37 0.9	06:48 5.4	19:05 5.6
15 Wed	07:28 6.8	19:56 6.9	02:06 0.9	14:32 0.9	07:39 5.0	20:09 5.0	02:08 0.8	14:30 0.7	07:32 5.6	19:58 5.6
16 Thu	08:14 6.9	20:51 6.8	02:54 0.8	15:25 0.7	08:24 5.0	21:05 5.0	02:56 0.8	15:24 0.6	08:17 5.6	20:52 5.6
17 Fri	09:00 6.8	21:47 6.7	03:40 0.9	16:16 0.6	09:11 5.0	22:00 4.9	03:43 0.9	16:21 0.6	09:04 5.6	21:46 5.5
18 Sat	09:46 6.7	22:42 6.4	04:30 1.1	17:07 0.6	09:59 4.9	22:57 4.4	04:30 1.1	17:18 0.7	09:51 5.5	22:43 5.3
19 Sun	10:35 6.5	23:39 6.1	05:09 1.4	17:58 0.7	10:50 4.8	23:57 4.4	05:17 1.3	18:15 0.8	10:41 5.4	23:46 5.1
20 Mon	11:28 6.2		05:54 1.8	18:51 0.9	11:47 4.7		06:07 1.5	19:13 0.9	11:35 5.2	
21 Tue ◐	00:38 5.8	12:30 6.0	06:45 2.0	19:49 1.2	01:02 4.2	12:51 4.5	07:02 1.7	20:12 1.1	00:53 4.9	12:35 5.0
22 Wed	01:41 5.6	13:39 5.8	07:44 2.2	20:51 1.4	02:08 4.1	13:59 4.4	08:03 1.8	21:12 1.2	02:00 4.7	13:44 4.9
23 Thu	02:46 5.5	14:48 5.8	08:53 2.3	21:54 1.6	03:12 4.0	15:06 4.3	09:10 1.9	22:12 1.3	03:02 4.7	14:54 4.8
24 Fri	03:48 5.6	15:53 5.8	10:02 2.2	22:51 1.6	04:11 4.0	16:07 4.3	10:17 1.8	23:06 1.4	03:59 4.7	15:58 4.8
25 Sat	04:42 5.8	16:50 5.9	11:03 2.0	23:40 1.7	05:01 4.1	17:03 4.3	11:18 1.7	23:54 1.4	04:50 4.8	16:55 4.8
26 Sun	05:29 6.0	17:39 5.9	11:54 1.8		05:43 4.3	17:53 4.4		12:10 1.5	05:35 4.9	17:44 4.9
27 Mon	06:10 6.2	18:24 6.0	00:21 1.7	12:39 1.7	06:21 4.4	18:38 4.4	00:36 1.4	12:57 1.4	06:13 5.0	18:28 5.0
28 Tue	06:47 6.3	19:06 6.0	00:56 1.6	13:20 1.6	06:57 4.6	19:20 4.4	01:13 1.3	13:41 1.3	06:50 5.1	19:09 5.1
29 Wed ●	07:21 6.3	19:45 6.1	01:29 1.6	13:59 1.5	07:33 4.6	20:00 4.5	01:48 1.3	14:21 1.2	07:24 5.2	19:47 5.1
30 Thu	07:52 6.4	20:24 6.1	02:02 1.6	14:36 1.5	08:07 4.7	20:37 4.5	02:24 1.3	14:57 1.1	07:58 5.3	20:25 5.1

Tidal information computed by POLTIPS software developed by National Oceanography Centre

June 2022

Times: GMT / BST

Heights: metres (above chart datum)

		WINTERTON				GORLESTON				WELLS BAR	
		HW AM	HW PM	LW AM	LW PM	HW AM	HW PM	LW AM	LW PM	HW AM	HW PM
1 Wed		09:17 3.2	21:46 2.9	03:47 1.0	16:14 0.9	11:06 2.4	23:23 2.2	04:50 0.9	17:18 0.8	08:11 5.6	20:32 5.5
2 Thu		09:45 3.2	22:25 2.8	04:12 1.1	16:49 0.9	11:06 2.4	23:39 2.2	05:00 0.9	17:42 0.8	08:43 5.6	21:08 5.3
3 Fri		10:15 3.2	23:04 2.7	04:36 1.2	17:25 0.9	11:36 2.5		05:24 1.0	18:12 0.8	09:14 5.5	21:44 5.2
4 Sat		10:49 3.1	23:47 2.6	05:05 1.3	18:05 0.9	00:13 2.2	12:17 2.5	06:00 1.0	18:51 0.8	09:48 5.3	22:23 5.0
5 Sun		11:28 3.0		05:44 1.4	18:50 1.0	00:58 2.1	13:06 2.4	06:43 1.1	19:42 0.8	10:26 5.2	23:06 4.9
6 Mon		00:36 2.6	12:13 2.9	06:32 1.5	19:41 1.0	01:53 2.1	14:04 2.3	07:33 1.2	20:40 0.8	11:09 5.0	23:59 4.7
7 Tue	●	01:32 2.5	13:05 2.8	07:30 1.6	20:38 1.0	02:56 2.0	15:08 2.3	08:35 1.2	21:43 0.8		12:02 4.9
8 Wed		02:38 2.5	14:04 2.8	08:41 1.6	21:41 1.0	04:05 2.0	16:13 2.2	09:44 1.3	22:51 0.8	01:01 4.7	13:05 4.8
9 Thu		03:42 2.6	15:14 2.8	09:56 1.6	22:41 0.9	05:18 2.1	17:18 2.2	10:58 1.3	23:55 0.7	02:11 4.7	14:15 4.9
10 Fri		04:38 2.8	16:19 2.9	11:00 1.5	23:38 0.8	06:24 2.1	18:20 2.3		12:08 1.2	03:14 4.9	15:19 5.1
11 Sat		05:28 2.9	17:18 3.1	11:57 1.3		07:19 2.2	19:15 2.4	00:52 0.6	13:08 1.1	04:11 5.1	16:17 5.4
12 Sun		06:16 3.0	18:10 3.2	00:31 0.7	12:50 1.2	08:09 2.3	20:06 2.4	01:44 0.5	14:01 0.9	05:04 5.4	17:11 5.6
13 Mon		07:01 3.2	19:04 3.4	01:22 0.7	13:44 1.0	08:55 2.4	20:57 2.5	02:33 0.5	14:52 0.8	05:53 5.6	18:05 5.8
14 Tue	○	07:44 3.3	19:59 3.5	02:12 0.6	14:38 0.8	09:39 2.4	21:51 2.5	03:21 0.5	15:45 0.7	06:41 5.8	18:59 5.9
15 Wed		08:28 3.4	20:55 3.5	03:02 0.7	15:32 0.6	10:23 2.5	22:48 2.6	04:07 0.5	16:39 0.6	07:26 5.9	19:53 6.0
16 Thu		09:13 3.5	21:51 3.5	03:50 0.8	16:25 0.5	11:06 2.6	23:48 2.5	04:54 0.6	17:33 0.5	08:12 5.9	20:47 5.9
17 Fri		09:58 3.5	22:44 3.4	04:38 0.9	17:16 0.4	11:52 2.6		05:41 0.8	18:26 0.4	08:59 5.9	21:40 5.8
18 Sat		10:43 3.5	23:39 3.2	05:26 1.0	18:08 0.4	00:45 2.5	12:40 2.6	06:29 0.9	19:18 0.4	09:45 5.8	22:35 5.6
19 Sun		11:30 3.4		06:14 1.4	19:00 0.4	01:40 2.4	13:31 2.6	07:18 1.0	20:11 0.4	10:33 5.7	23:35 5.4
20 Mon	●	00:37 3.0	12:18 3.4	07:05 1.4	19:56 0.5	02:36 2.4	14:23 2.6	08:09 1.2	21:06 0.5	11:25 5.5	
21 Tue		01:46 2.9	13:10 3.2	07:59 1.5	20:56 0.6	03:36 2.3	15:17 2.6	09:01 1.2	22:04 0.5	00:40 5.2	12:22 5.4
22 Wed		03:01 2.8	14:11 3.1	09:03 1.6	22:01 0.8	04:43 2.2	16:14 2.5	09:59 1.3	23:06 0.6	01:45 5.0	13:29 5.2
23 Thu		04:10 2.8	15:23 3.0	10:14 1.6	23:06 0.9	05:51 2.2	17:15 2.4	11:03 1.3		02:47 5.0	14:39 5.1
24 Fri		05:10 2.8	16:23 3.0	11:22 1.5		06:52 2.2	18:19 2.4	00:09 0.7	12:12 1.2	03:45 5.0	15:44 5.1
25 Sat		06:02 2.9	17:49 2.9	00:05 1.0	12:23 1.4	07:45 2.3	19:21 2.3	01:07 0.8	13:22 1.1	04:38 5.0	16:43 5.2
26 Sun		06:45 3.0	18:48 2.9	00:56 1.1	13:17 1.2	08:32 2.3	20:22 2.3	01:59 0.8	14:24 1.0	05:25 5.2	17:35 5.2
27 Mon		07:23 3.1	19:38 2.9	01:38 1.1	14:03 1.1	09:12 2.4	21:20 2.3	02:44 0.9	15:14 0.9	06:05 5.3	18:20 5.3
28 Tue		07:57 3.2	20:23 2.9	02:17 1.1	14:46 1.0	09:48 2.4	22:08 2.3	03:22 0.9	15:57 0.8	06:43 5.4	19:03 5.4
29 Wed	●	08:28 3.3	21:03 2.9	02:50 1.1	15:26 0.9	10:15 2.4	22:47 2.2	03:50 1.0	16:36 0.8	07:18 5.5	19:42 5.4
30 Thu		08:57 3.3	21:39 2.9	03:20 1.2	16:02 0.9	10:13 2.5	23:11 2.2	04:04 1.0	17:07 0.7	07:53 5.6	20:20 5.4

Tidal information computed by POLTIPS software developed by National Oceanography Centre

July 2022

Times: GMT / BST

Heights: metres (above chart datum)

Day	HUNSTANTON HW AM	HW PM	LW AM	LW PM	CROMER/SHERINGHAM HW AM	HW PM	LW AM	LW PM	BLAKENEY BAR HW AM	HW PM
1 Fri	08:22 6.4	21:01 6.2	02:37 1.5	15:13 1.4	08:40 4.7	21:14 4.4	02:58 1.3	15:33 1.1	08:31 5.3	21:00 5.0
2 Sat	08:52 6.4	21:39 6.1	03:12 1.5	15:51 1.4	09:12 4.7	21:51 4.4	03:32 1.3	16:09 1.1	09:04 5.3	21:36 5.0
3 Sun	09:24 6.3	22:16 6.0	03:49 1.6	16:29 1.4	09:44 4.6	22:28 4.3	04:07 1.4	16:45 1.1	09:40 5.2	22:13 4.9
4 Mon	09:59 6.2	22:55 5.8	04:26 1.7	17:07 1.4	10:18 4.6	23:09 4.2	04:43 1.5	17:24 1.2	10:16 5.1	22:53 4.8
5 Tue	10:39 6.1	23:39 5.6	05:03 1.8	17:47 1.6	10:57 4.5	23:54 4.1	05:20 1.6	18:05 1.3	10:56 5.0	23:37 4.7
6 Wed	11:26 6.0		05:45 2.0	18:30 1.7	11:42 4.4		06:02 1.7	18:51 1.3	11:39 4.9	
7 Thu ◐	00:28 5.5	12:23 5.9	06:31 2.2	19:18 1.8	00:45 4.0	12:37 4.4	06:51 1.8	19:44 1.4	00:28 4.6	12:30 4.8
8 Fri	01:25 5.4	13:28 5.8	07:26 2.3	20:15 1.8	01:44 4.0	13:41 4.3	07:51 1.9	20:44 1.4	01:28 4.6	13:33 4.8
9 Sat	02:28 5.4	14:36 5.9	08:31 2.3	21:24 1.8	02:47 4.0	14:49 4.3	09:00 1.9	21:51 1.4	02:35 4.6	14:44 4.8
10 Sun	03:33 5.6	15:45 6.0	09:46 2.2	22:38 1.7	03:51 4.2	16:00 4.4	10:12 1.7	23:00 1.3	03:40 4.7	15:53 5.0
11 Mon	04:35 5.9	16:53 6.2	11:03 1.9	23:47 1.5	04:52 4.4	17:09 4.6	11:22 1.5		04:42 4.9	16:59 5.1
12 Tue	05:33 6.2	17:58 6.5		12:16 1.6	05:47 4.6	18:13 4.8	00:03 1.2	12:26 1.2	05:41 5.2	18:03 5.3
13 Wed ○	06:26 6.5	19:00 6.7	00:50 1.3	13:24 1.3	06:37 4.8	19:12 4.9	01:01 1.0	13:27 1.0	06:33 5.4	19:02 5.5
14 Thu	07:17 6.8	19:57 6.9	01:49 1.1	14:28 0.9	07:26 5.0	20:06 5.0	01:54 1.0	14:28 0.7	07:21 5.6	19:56 5.6
15 Fri	08:04 7.0	20:51 7.0	02:43 1.0	15:25 0.6	08:13 5.1	21:00 5.0	02:45 0.9	15:30 0.5	08:07 5.7	20:49 5.6
16 Sat	08:49 7.0	21:40 6.9	03:32 1.0	16:15 0.4	09:00 5.2	21:51 4.9	03:33 0.9	16:26 0.4	08:52 5.8	21:40 5.6
17 Sun	09:33 7.0	22:27 6.7	04:16 1.1	17:01 0.3	09:45 5.1	22:40 4.8	04:18 1.0	17:16 0.5	09:38 5.8	22:31 5.4
18 Mon	10:16 6.9	23:12 6.4	04:56 1.2	17:44 0.5	10:30 5.1	23:28 4.5	05:01 1.1	18:01 0.6	10:22 5.7	23:20 5.2
19 Tue	11:02 6.6	23:58 6.0	05:33 1.5	18:26 0.9	11:18 4.9		05:42 1.3	18:45 0.8	11:08 5.5	
20 Wed ◐	11:52 6.3		06:12 1.8	19:09 1.3	00:18 4.3	12:09 4.7	06:27 1.5	19:28 1.1	00:11 5.0	*11:58 5.2
21 Thu	00:49 5.7	12:51 6.0	06:57 2.0	19:56 1.7	01:12 4.1	13:09 4.4	07:16 1.8	20:16 1.4	01:04 4.7	12:53 5.0
22 Fri	01:48 5.4	14:00 5.6	07:53 2.3	20:54 2.1	02:13 3.9	14:19 4.2	08:17 1.9	21:15 1.6	02:02 4.5	14:01 4.7
23 Sat	02:56 5.3	15:15 5.5	09:06 2.4	21:57 2.2	03:19 3.9	15:33 4.1	09:30 2.0	22:19 1.8	03:05 4.5	15:16 4.6
24 Sun	04:03 5.4	16:25 5.5	10:21 2.3	22:56 2.2	04:21 4.0	16:42 4.1	10:45 1.9	23:19 1.8	04:08 4.5	16:28 4.6
25 Mon	05:01 5.6	17:24 5.6	11:24 2.2	23:43 2.1	05:15 4.1	17:39 4.1	11:49 1.8		05:04 4.6	17:28 4.7
26 Tue	05:48 5.9	18:15 5.8		12:15 2.0	06:00 4.3	18:27 4.2	00:09 1.7	12:42 1.5	05:51 4.8	18:17 4.8
27 Wed	06:29 6.1	18:58 6.0	00:25 2.0	13:02 1.8	06:39 4.5	19:07 4.4	00:51 1.5	13:26 1.4	06:30 5.0	18:57 5.0
28 Thu ●	07:04 6.3	19:38 6.2	01:05 1.8	13:47 1.6	07:16 4.6	19:44 4.5	01:29 1.5	14:06 1.2	07:07 5.2	19:34 5.1
29 Fri	07:36 6.4	20:15 6.4	01:45 1.6	14:30 1.4	07:50 4.8	20:19 4.6	02:05 1.4	14:45 1.1	07:40 5.3	20:09 5.1
30 Sat	08:07 6.5	20:50 6.5	02:26 1.5	15:12 1.3	08:23 4.8	20:54 4.6	02:41 1.3	15:22 1.0	08:13 5.4	20:42 5.2

Tidal information computed by POLTIPS software developed by National Oceanography Centre

July 2022

Times: GMT / BST

Heights: metres (above chart datum)

		WINTERTON				GORLESTON				WELLS BAR	
		HW AM	HW PM	LW AM	LW PM	HW AM	HW PM	LW AM	LW PM	HW AM	HW PM
1	Fri	09:26 3.3	22:13 2.8	03:46 1.2	16:39 0.8	10:39 2.6	23:23 2.2	04:30 1.0	17:36 0.7	08:26 5.6	20:55 5.4
2	Sat	09:58 3.4	22:48 2.8	04:14 1.2	17:15 0.8	11:20 2.6		05:06 1.0	18:10 0.7	08:59 5.6	21:30 5.3
3	Sun	10:32 3.3	23:24 2.8	04:47 1.2	17:53 0.8	00:03 2.2	12:06 2.6	05:47 1.0	18:50 0.7	09:34 5.5	22:06 5.3
4	Mon	11:10 3.3		05:26 1.3	18:32 0.8	00:49 2.2	12:56 2.5	06:31 1.0	19:34 0.7	10:09 5.4	22:45 5.1
5	Tue	00:03 2.7	*11:47 3.2	06:08 1.3	19:14 0.9	01:39 2.2	13:47 2.5	07:18 1.1	20:21 0.7	10:47 5.3	23:27 5.0
6	Wed	00:46 2.7	12:30 3.1	06:56 1.4	20:01 0.9	02:31 2.1	14:38 2.4	08:09 1.1	21:13 0.8	11:29 5.2	
7	Thu ◑	01:39 2.6	13:18 3.1	07:53 1.5	20:55 0.9	03:29 2.1	15:30 2.4	09:05 1.2	22:12 0.8	00:16 4.9	12:18 5.2
8	Fri	02:45 2.7	14:20 3.0	08:59 1.5	21:56 0.9	04:36 2.1	16:28 2.4	10:10 1.3	23:16 0.8	01:14 4.9	13:19 5.1
9	Sat	03:50 2.8	15:35 3.0	10:14 1.5	23:00 0.9	05:44 2.2	17:39 2.4	11:27 1.2		02:20 4.9	14:29 5.1
10	Sun	04:48 2.9	16:44 3.1	11:23 1.4		06:49 2.2	18:46 2.4	00:18 0.8	12:37 1.2	03:26 5.0	15:39 5.2
11	Mon	05:42 3.0	17:47 3.2	00:00 0.9	12:26 1.2	07:41 2.3	19:45 2.4	01:15 0.7	13:38 1.0	04:30 5.2	16:48 5.4
12	Tue	06:34 3.1	18:51 3.3	00:57 0.9	13:29 1.0	08:29 2.4	20:42 2.4	02:06 0.7	14:37 0.9	05:31 5.4	17:55 5.6
13	Wed ○	07:25 3.3	19:58 3.4	01:53 0.9	14:31 0.8	09:15 2.5	21:46 2.5	02:57 0.7	15:38 0.7	06:26 5.7	18:56 5.8
14	Thu	08:13 3.5	20:55 3.5	02:47 0.9	15:28 0.6	10:01 2.6	22:51 2.6	03:49 0.7	16:36 0.5	07:15 5.9	19:51 5.9
15	Fri	08:59 3.6	21:46 3.5	03:38 0.9	16:19 0.4	10:50 2.7	23:47 2.6	04:41 0.8	17:28 0.3	08:02 6.0	20:44 5.9
16	Sat	09:44 3.8	22:34 3.4	04:26 1.0	17:07 0.3	11:39 2.8		05:30 0.8	18:17 0.2	08:47 6.1	21:34 5.9
17	Sun	10:27 3.8	23:21 3.2	05:11 1.0	17:53 0.3	00:36 2.6	12:27 2.8	06:16 0.9	19:04 0.2	09:32 6.1	22:23 5.7
18	Mon	11:10 3.8		05:53 1.1	18:39 0.4	01:24 2.5	13:14 2.8	07:00 1.0	19:51 0.3	10:15 6.0	23:10 5.5
19	Tue ◐	00:00 3.0	*11:53 3.6	06:36 1.3	19:26 0.5	02:12 2.4	14:01 2.8	07:43 1.0	20:39 0.4	10:59 5.8	23:59 5.2
20	Wed	01:05 3.0	12:40 3.4	07:21 1.4	20:16 0.7	03:01 2.3	14:50 2.7	08:28 1.1	21:29 0.6	11:47 5.5	
21	Thu	02:09 2.7	13:33 3.2	08:12 1.5	21:12 1.0	03:57 2.2	15:41 2.6	09:18 1.2	22:25 0.8	00:50 5.0	12:40 5.2
22	Fri	03:17 2.7	14:42 3.0	09:16 1.6	22:20 1.1	05:01 2.2	16:39 2.4	10:18 1.3	23:27 0.9	01:47 4.8	13:46 5.0
23	Sat	04:22 2.7	16:02 2.8	10:39 1.6	23:26 1.2	06:08 2.2	17:45 2.3	11:36 1.3		02:50 4.8	15:01 4.8
24	Sun	05:25 2.8	17:36 2.8	11:58 1.4		07:07 2.2	19:00 2.2	00:30 1.0	13:03 1.2	03:55 4.8	16:15 4.8
25	Mon	06:18 2.9	18:45 2.8	00:25 1.3	13:01 1.3	07:59 2.3	20:21 2.2	01:27 1.1	14:13 1.1	04:53 5.0	17:18 5.0
26	Tue	07:01 3.1	19:34 2.9	01:15 1.3	13:51 1.1	08:42 2.4	21:07 2.2	02:16 1.1	15:03 1.0	05:42 5.2	18:09 5.1
27	Wed	07:36 3.2	20:10 2.9	01:56 1.3	14:34 1.0	09:15 2.4	22:04 2.3	02:54 1.1	15:45 0.8	06:23 5.3	18:51 5.3
28	Thu ●	08:07 3.3	20:51 3.0	02:32 1.3	15:12 0.9	09:27 2.5	22:39 2.3	03:17 1.1	16:20 0.7	07:01 5.5	19:29 5.4
29	Fri	08:37 3.4	21:23 3.0	03:01 1.2	15:48 0.8	09:48 2.6	23:06 2.3	03:42 1.0	16:51 0.7	07:35 5.6	20:04 5.4
30	Sat	09:08 3.5	21:53 3.0	03:29 1.2	16:23 0.8	10:29 2.6	23:30 2.3	04:20 1.0	17:24 0.6	08:08 5.7	20:37 5.5
31	Sun	09:41 3.6	22:24 3.0	03:59 1.2	16:58 0.7	11:14 2.7		04:57 0.9	17:58 0.6	08:41 5.8	21:11 5.5

©Bittern Books. Reproduction strictly prohibited.

Tidal information computed by POLTIPS software developed by National Oceanography Centre

Times: GMT / BST — August 2022 — Heights: metres (above chart datum)

Day		HUNSTANTON HW AM	HW PM	LW AM	LW PM	CROMER/SHERINGHAM HW AM	HW PM	LW AM	LW PM	BLAKENEY BAR HW AM	HW PM
1 Mon		09:07 6.7	21:54 6.4	03:43 1.4	16:27 1.2	09:24 4.9	22:03 4.6	03:51 1.2	16:31 1.0	09:20 5.4	21:50 5.2
2 Tue		09:39 6.7	22:27 6.3	04:18 1.4	17:00 1.2	09:54 4.8	22:39 4.5	04:24 1.3	17:03 1.0	09:53 5.4	22:26 5.1
3 Wed		10:15 6.6	23:01 6.0	04:51 1.6	17:31 1.4	10:27 4.8	23:18 4.4	04:57 1.4	17:36 1.1	10:29 5.3	23:05 5.0
4 Thu		10:56 6.4	23:42 5.8	05:23 1.8	18:03 1.6	11:07 4.7		05:33 1.5	18:12 1.2	11:06 5.2	23:47 4.8
5 Fri	◐	11:46 6.2		06:00 2.0	18:42 1.8	00:03 4.3	*11:57 4.6	06:15 1.6	18:58 1.3	11:52 5.1	
6 Sat		00:33 5.6	12:48 5.9	06:47 2.2	19:33 2.0	00:56 4.1	13:00 4.4	07:09 1.8	19:57 1.5	00:39 4.7	12:50 4.9
7 Sun		01:39 5.4	14:03 5.8	07:51 2.3	20:47 2.1	02:02 4.0	14:18 4.3	08:19 1.9	21:13 1.6	01:46 4.6	14:08 4.8
8 Mon		02:57 5.5	15:31 5.8	09:18 2.3	22:15 2.0	03:19 4.1	15:51 4.3	09:42 1.8	22:39 1.6	03:05 4.6	15:34 4.8
9 Tue		04:16 5.7	16:54 6.0	10:52 2.1	23:34 1.8	04:33 4.2	17:11 4.4	11:09 1.6	23:52 1.4	04:22 4.8	16:58 5.0
10 Wed		05:22 6.1	18:04 6.4		12:15 1.6	05:36 4.5	18:15 4.7		12:21 1.2	05:29 5.1	18:07 5.2
11 Thu		06:18 6.5	19:03 6.9	00:42 1.5	13:27 1.2	06:28 4.8	19:10 4.9	00:51 1.2	13:27 0.9	06:24 5.4	19:02 5.5
12 Fri	○	07:08 6.9	19:54 7.1	01:43 1.2	14:28 0.7	07:16 5.1	20:00 5.0	01:43 1.1	14:30 0.6	07:10 5.6	19:52 5.6
13 Sat		07:52 7.2	20:40 7.2	02:36 1.0	15:19 0.3	08:00 5.2	20:47 5.1	02:32 1.0	15:27 0.4	07:52 5.8	20:37 5.7
14 Sun		08:33 7.3	21:21 7.2	03:21 0.9	16:03 0.2	08:43 5.4	21:30 5.0	03:18 0.9	16:14 0.3	08:34 6.0	21:21 5.6
15 Mon		09:12 7.4	22:00 7.0	04:00 0.9	16:43 0.3	09:24 5.4	22:10 4.8	03:58 0.9	16:55 0.4	09:16 6.0	22:03 5.5
16 Tue		09:51 7.2	22:36 6.6	04:34 1.0	17:18 0.6	10:03 5.2	22:49 4.6	04:36 1.0	17:30 0.6	09:56 5.8	22:40 5.3
17 Wed		10:30 6.9	23:14 6.2	05:05 1.2	17:50 1.0	10:43 5.0	23:28 4.4	05:11 1.2	18:02 0.9	10:37 5.6	23:17 5.0
18 Thu		11:13 6.5	23:55 5.8	05:36 1.6	18:21 1.5	11:27 4.8		05:48 1.4	18:33 1.3	11:19 5.3	
19 Fri	●		12:03 6.0	06:12 1.9	18:56 2.1	00:12 4.2	12:20 4.4	06:30 1.7	19:13 1.6		12:05 4.9
20 Sat		00:45 5.4	13:06 5.4	07:00 2.3	19:43 2.5	01:08 3.9	13:31 4.0	07:25 2.0	20:09 2.0	00:47 4.5	13:07 4.5
21 Sun		01:54 5.1	14:35 5.1	08:08 2.7	20:54 2.8	02:23 3.8	15:05 3.8	08:42 2.2	21:27 2.2	01:55 4.3	14:32 4.3
22 Mon		03:22 5.1	16:07 5.1	09:40 2.7	22:13 2.7	03:43 3.8	16:26 3.8	10:17 2.1	22:49 2.1	03:20 4.3	16:06 4.3
23 Tue		04:36 5.3	17:14 5.4	11:00 2.5	23:15 2.5	04:48 4.0	17:28 4.0	11:32 1.9	23:48 2.0	04:35 4.5	17:15 4.5
24 Wed		05:28 5.7	18:04 5.8		12:00 2.2	05:39 4.4	18:14 4.4		12:26 1.6	05:30 4.7	18:03 4.8
25 Thu		06:09 6.0	18:45 6.1	00:04 2.2	12:50 1.8	06:21 4.5	18:51 4.4	00:32 1.8	13:10 1.4	06:10 5.0	18:42 5.0
26 Fri		06:44 6.4	19:23 6.5	00:49 1.8	13:36 1.5	06:56 4.7	19:24 4.6	01:10 1.6	13:49 1.2	06:46 5.2	19:16 5.2
27 Sat	●	07:16 6.6	19:57 6.7	01:33 1.5	14:21 1.2	07:28 4.8	19:55 4.7	01:46 1.4	14:27 1.0	07:19 5.4	19:47 5.3
28 Sun		07:47 6.8	20:29 6.9	02:15 1.3	15:02 1.0	07:59 5.0	20:27 4.8	02:21 1.2	15:02 0.9	07:50 5.5	20:19 5.4
29 Mon		08:16 7.0	20:58 6.9	02:56 1.2	15:38 0.9	08:28 5.0	21:01 4.8	02:57 1.1	15:36 0.8	08:22 5.6	20:50 5.4
30 Tue		08:45 7.1	21:27 6.8	03:33 1.2	16:12 0.9	08:57 5.1	21:34 4.8	03:30 1.1	16:07 0.8	08:55 5.7	21:23 5.4

Tidal information computed by POLTIPS software developed by National Oceanography Centre

Times: GMT / BST

August 2022

Heights: metres (above chart datum)

Day	Moon	WINTERTON HW AM		WINTERTON HW PM		WINTERTON LW AM		WINTERTON LW PM		GORLESTON HW AM		GORLESTON HW PM		GORLESTON LW AM		GORLESTON LW PM		WELLS BAR HW AM		WELLS BAR HW PM	
1 Mon		10:13	3.6	22:55	2.9	04:33	1.2	17:32	0.7	00:02	2.3	12:00	2.7	05:39	0.9	18:36	0.6	09:14	5.8	21:44	5.5
2 Tue		10:47	3.5	23:30	2.9	05:09	1.2	18:08	0.7	00:39	2.3	12:42	2.6	06:18	0.9	19:15	0.6	09:47	5.7	22:19	5.4
3 Wed		11:21	3.5			05:46	1.2	18:44	0.8	01:19	2.3	13:21	2.6	06:57	1.0	19:55	0.7	10:21	5.6	22:56	5.3
4 Thu	◗	00:07	2.8	*11:59	3.4	06:26	1.3	19:25	0.8	02:00	2.2	13:59	2.6	07:36	1.1	20:39	0.8	10:57	5.5	23:36	5.1
5 Fri		00:52	2.8	12:43	3.3	07:14	1.4	20:14	0.9	02:46	2.2	14:36	2.5	08:18	1.2	21:30	0.9	11:41	5.4		
6 Sat		01:51	2.8	13:43	3.2	08:14	1.4	21:15	1.0	03:43	2.1	15:18	2.4	09:12	1.2	22:33	1.0	00:26	5.0	12:37	5.2
7 Sun		03:03	2.8	15:04	3.1	09:32	1.5	22:29	1.1	05:03	2.1	16:28	2.4	10:45	1.3	23:43	1.0	01:31	4.9	13:53	5.0
8 Mon		04:12	2.8	16:22	3.1	10:58	1.4	23:38	1.1	06:15	2.2	18:27	2.3			12:13	1.2	02:50	4.9	15:20	5.1
9 Tue		05:13	3.0	17:38	3.2			12:13	1.2	07:12	2.3	19:37	2.4	00:48	1.0	13:24	1.0	04:09	5.1	16:47	5.2
10 Wed		06:14	3.1	19:01	3.3	00:41	1.1	13:25	1.0	08:00	2.4	20:48	2.4	01:45	1.0	14:32	0.8	05:19	5.4	17:59	5.5
11 Thu	○	07:09	3.4	20:01	3.4	01:43	1.1	14:27	0.7	08:48	2.6	21:55	2.5	02:41	1.0	15:34	0.6	06:16	5.7	18:56	5.8
12 Fri		07:57	3.6	20:48	3.5	02:38	1.1	15:20	0.5	09:37	2.7	22:48	2.6	03:37	0.9	16:27	0.4	07:04	5.9	19:47	6.0
13 Sat		08:42	3.8	21:32	3.5	03:26	1.0	16:06	0.3	10:29	2.8	23:33	2.6	04:28	0.8	17:14	0.2	07:47	6.1	20:32	6.0
14 Sun		09:24	4.0	22:14	3.4	04:10	1.0	16:50	0.2	11:19	2.9			05:13	0.8	17:58	0.2	08:29	6.2	21:15	6.0
15 Mon		10:06	4.0	22:55	3.2	04:50	1.0	17:31	0.3	00:16	2.6	12:06	3.0	05:55	0.8	18:41	0.2	09:11	6.2	21:56	5.8
16 Tue		10:46	4.0	23:36	3.1	05:27	1.1	18:11	0.4	00:58	2.6	12:51	2.9	06:36	0.8	19:23	0.4	09:50	6.1	22:32	5.6
17 Wed		11:26	3.8			06:05	1.2	18:51	0.7	01:40	2.4	13:35	2.8	07:15	0.9	20:06	0.6	10:29	5.9	23:08	5.3
18 Thu		00:19	2.9	12:08	3.5	06:44	1.3	19:32	0.9	02:23	2.4	14:20	2.7	07:54	1.1	20:50	0.8	11:09	5.6	23:47	5.0
19 Fri	◐	01:07	2.8	12:59	3.2	07:29	1.4	20:20	1.2	03:09	2.3	15:07	2.5	08:36	1.2	21:38	1.0	11:54	5.2		
20 Sat		02:06	2.7	14:06	2.9	08:27	1.5	21:23	1.4	04:00	2.2	16:01	2.4	09:32	1.3	22:35	1.2	00:34	4.8	12:53	4.8
21 Sun		03:15	2.7	15:35	2.7	09:52	1.6	22:50	1.5	05:01	2.2	17:10	2.2	11:00	1.4	23:45	1.3	01:40	4.6	14:17	4.6
22 Mon		04:28	2.8	17:27	2.7	11:38	1.5			06:06	2.2	18:58	2.1			12:51	1.3	03:05	4.6	15:53	4.6
23 Tue		05:40	2.9	18:36	2.8	00:03	1.5	12:44	1.5	07:02	2.3	20:21	2.2	00:55	1.4	13:57	1.1	04:23	4.8	17:04	4.8
24 Wed		06:32	3.0	19:22	3.0	00:58	1.5	13:34	1.1	07:43	2.4	21:09	2.3	01:53	1.3	14:42	0.9	05:20	5.0	17:55	5.1
25 Thu		07:09	3.2	19:58	3.0	01:40	1.5	14:14	1.0	08:15	2.4	21:47	2.3	02:32	1.2	15:19	0.8	06:02	5.3	18:35	5.3
26 Fri		07:40	3.4	20:29	3.1	02:13	1.4	14:50	0.9	08:51	2.5	22:18	2.4	02:59	1.2	15:52	0.7	06:39	5.5	19:10	5.4
27 Sat	●	08:10	3.5	20:57	3.2	02:41	1.3	15:24	0.8	09:33	2.6	22:44	2.4	03:31	1.0	16:24	0.6	07:13	5.7	19:42	5.6
28 Sun		08:42	3.6	21:25	3.2	03:10	1.2	15:58	0.7	10:18	2.6	23:12	2.4	04:09	0.9	16:59	0.5	07:45	5.8	20:14	5.7
29 Mon		09:16	3.7	21:54	3.2	03:42	1.1	16:32	0.6	11:01	2.7	23:44	2.4	04:48	0.8	17:35	0.4	08:17	5.9	20:45	5.7
30 Tue		09:48	3.8	22:25	3.2	04:16	1.1	17:05	0.6	11:42	2.7			05:25	0.8	18:11	0.5	08:50	6.0	21:17	5.7
31 Wed		10:21	3.7	22:57	3.1	04:50	1.1	17:38	0.7	00:18	2.4	12:18	2.7	06:00	0.8	18:47	0.6	09:21	5.9	21:50	5.6

Tidal information computed by POLTIPS software developed by National Oceanography Centre

September 2022

Times: GMT / BST

Heights: metres (above chart datum)

©Bittern Books. Reproduction strictly prohibited.

Day	HUNSTANTON HW AM	HW PM	LW AM	LW PM	CROMER/SHERINGHAM HW AM	HW PM	LW AM	LW PM	BLAKENEY BAR HW AM	HW PM
1 Thu	09:50 7.0	22:26 6.4	04:36 1.4	17:10 1.3	10:00 5.0	22:45 4.6	04:33 1.2	17:05 1.0	10:01 5.5	22:31 5.2
2 Fri	10:30 6.7	23:05 6.1	05:05 1.6	17:39 1.6	10:39 4.9	23:26 4.4	05:06 1.3	17:39 1.2	10:37 5.4	23:11 5.0
3 Sat ◗	11:18 6.3	23:55 5.8	05:38 1.9	18:14 1.9	11:30 4.6		05:47 1.5	18:24 1.4	11:23 5.1	
4 Sun		12:22 5.8	06:25 2.1	19:07 2.2	00:18 4.2	12:37 4.3	06:42 1.7	19:26 1.7	00:00 4.8	12:23 4.8
5 Mon	01:05 5.4	13:54 5.5	07:36 2.4	20:30 2.5	01:29 4.0	14:15 4.1	07:57 1.9	20:54 1.9	01:09 4.6	13:53 4.6
6 Tue	02:40 5.4	15:42 5.6	09:19 2.4	22:11 2.4	03:03 4.0	16:01 4.2	09:37 1.8	22:33 1.9	02:41 4.5	15:40 4.6
7 Wed	04:09 5.7	17:04 6.0	11:02 2.0	23:33 2.0	04:25 4.2	17:18 4.4	11:12 1.5	23:45 1.6	04:13 4.7	17:07 4.9
8 Thu	05:15 6.2	18:06 6.5		12:21 1.4	05:28 4.6	18:15 4.7		12:24 1.1	05:21 5.1	18:07 5.3
9 Fri	06:09 6.7	18:57 7.0	00:39 1.6	13:24 0.8	06:18 4.9	19:03 4.9	00:40 1.4	13:26 0.8	06:11 5.4	18:56 5.6
10 Sat ○	06:54 7.1	19:40 7.3	01:33 1.2	14:16 0.4	07:01 5.2	19:45 5.1	01:28 1.1	14:21 0.5	06:54 5.7	19:38 5.7
11 Sun	07:35 7.4	20:19 7.4	02:20 1.0	15:01 0.2	07:42 5.4	20:24 5.1	02:13 1.0	15:08 0.4	07:34 5.9	20:16 5.7
12 Mon	08:12 7.6	20:54 7.3	03:00 0.8	15:40 0.2	08:20 5.4	21:01 5.0	02:54 0.9	15:48 0.4	08:12 6.0	20:52 5.7
13 Tue	08:48 7.6	21:27 7.1	03:35 0.8	16:14 0.4	08:57 5.4	21:35 4.9	03:32 0.9	16:21 0.6	08:49 6.0	21:26 5.5
14 Wed	09:23 7.4	21:59 6.8	04:05 1.0	16:42 0.8	09:33 5.3	22:07 4.7	04:06 1.0	16:48 0.8	09:28 5.8	22:00 5.3
15 Thu	09:59 7.0	22:30 6.4	04:33 1.2	17:07 1.3	10:09 5.0	22:41 4.5	04:39 1.1	17:11 1.1	10:05 5.6	22:31 5.1
16 Fri	10:36 6.5	23:04 6.0	05:00 1.5	17:30 1.8	10:50 4.7	23:18 4.3	05:11 1.4	17:37 1.4	10:42 5.2	23:05 4.9
17 Sat ◑	11:19 5.9	23:44 5.5	05:33 1.9	17:57 2.3	11:37 4.3		05:48 1.7	18:12 1.8	11:24 4.8	23:46 4.6
18 Sun		12:15 5.3	06:14 2.4	18:39 2.7	00:05 4.0	12:45 3.9	06:38 2.0	19:03 2.2		12:20 4.4
19 Mon	00:42 5.1	13:49 4.9	07:14 2.8	19:45 3.1	01:19 3.8	14:36 3.7	07:56 2.2	20:28 2.4	00:45 4.3	13:50 4.1
20 Tue	02:25 4.9	15:42 4.9	08:52 2.9	21:24 3.1	03:01 3.8	16:05 3.7	09:43 2.2	22:13 2.4	02:21 4.2	15:38 4.1
21 Wed	04:00 5.1	16:53 5.3	10:35 2.6	22:46 2.7	04:17 3.9	17:08 3.9	11:08 1.9	23:22 2.2	03:58 4.3	16:52 4.4
22 Thu	04:57 5.6	17:42 5.8	11:39 2.2	23:42 2.3	05:12 4.2	17:51 4.2		12:01 1.6	04:59 4.6	17:40 4.8
23 Fri	05:39 6.0	18:21 6.3		12:29 1.7	05:54 4.5	18:25 4.4	00:07 1.9	12:42 1.3	05:42 5.0	18:16 5.0
24 Sat	06:15 6.5	18:57 6.7	00:29 1.8	13:14 1.3	06:28 4.7	18:56 4.6	00:45 1.6	13:20 1.1	06:19 5.2	18:49 5.2
25 Sun ●	06:48 6.8	19:29 7.0	01:13 1.5	13:57 1.0	06:59 4.9	19:27 4.8	01:21 1.3	13:57 0.9	06:51 5.5	19:20 5.4
26 Mon	07:18 7.1	19:59 7.1	01:55 1.2	14:36 0.8	07:27 5.0	19:58 4.9	01:57 1.2	14:32 0.8	07:23 5.6	19:49 5.5
27 Tue	07:48 7.3	20:27 7.1	02:35 1.1	15:12 0.8	07:57 5.2	20:30 5.0	02:32 1.0	15:06 0.7	07:54 5.7	20:21 5.6
28 Wed	08:19 7.2	20:55 7.0	03:12 1.0	15:42 0.8	08:28 5.2	21:04 5.0	03:05 1.0	15:36 0.7	08:26 5.8	20:53 5.6
29 Thu	08:52 7.3	21:24 6.9	03:46 1.1	16:17 1.0	09:02 5.2	21:38 4.9	03:37 1.0	16:06 0.8	09:00 5.7	21:27 5.5
30 Fri	09:29 7.1	21:57 6.6	04:18 1.3	16:46 1.2	09:39 5.1	22:14 4.7	04:09 1.1	16:36 1.0	09:36 5.6	22:03 5.3

Tidal information computed by POLTIPS software developed by National Oceanography Centre

September 2022

Times: GMT / BST

Heights: metres (above chart datum)

		WINTERTON				GORLESTON				WELLS BAR	
		HW AM	HW PM	LW AM	LW PM	HW AM	HW PM	LW AM	LW PM	HW AM	HW PM
1 Thu		10:55 3.6	23:33 3.0	05:23 1.2	18:13 0.8	00:51 2.4	12:51 2.7	06:33 0.9	19:21 0.7	09:54 5.8	22:23 5.5
2 Fri		11:33 3.5		06:01 1.3	18:50 0.9	01:24 2.3	13:22 2.6	07:05 1.0	19:57 0.8	10:29 5.7	23:02 5.3
3 Sat	◐	00:15 3.0	12:19 3.4	06:46 1.3	19:38 1.1	02:01 2.3	14:02 2.5	07:43 1.1	20:42 1.0	11:13 5.4	23:49 5.1
4 Sun		01:09 2.9	13:25 3.2	07:45 1.4	20:42 1.3	02:49 2.2	15:00 2.4	08:36 1.2	21:47 1.2		12:11 5.1
5 Mon		02:20 2.8	14:52 3.1	09:08 1.4	22:08 1.4	03:59 2.2	16:36 2.3	10:21 1.1	23:09 1.3	00:55 4.8	13:38 4.9
6 Tue		03:37 2.8	16:22 3.1	10:47 1.3	23:28 1.4	05:30 2.2	18:29 2.3	11:59 1.1		02:26 4.8	15:26 4.9
7 Wed		04:47 3.0	17:59 3.2		12:10 1.1	06:36 2.3	19:51 2.4	00:25 1.3	13:18 0.9	04:00 5.0	16:56 5.2
8 Thu		05:53 3.2	19:05 3.4	00:35 1.4	13:21 0.8	07:30 2.5	21:00 2.5	01:30 1.2	14:26 0.7	05:11 5.4	17:59 5.6
9 Fri		06:49 3.5	19:52 3.5	01:35 1.3	14:17 0.6	08:18 2.6	21:49 2.6	02:31 1.1	15:21 0.5	06:03 5.8	18:50 5.8
10 Sat	○	07:37 3.7	20:32 3.5	02:25 1.2	15:04 0.4	09:10 2.7	22:31 2.6	03:24 1.0	16:08 0.3	06:47 6.0	19:33 6.0
11 Sun		08:20 4.0	21:11 3.5	03:08 1.0	15:46 0.3	10:04 2.9	23:10 2.6	04:09 0.8	16:51 0.2	07:28 6.2	20:11 6.0
12 Mon		09:02 4.1	21:48 3.4	03:47 1.0	16:25 0.3	10:55 2.9	23:48 2.6	04:51 0.8	17:33 0.2	08:07 6.3	20:47 6.0
13 Tue		09:42 4.1	22:25 3.3	04:23 1.0	17:02 0.4	11:42 2.9		05:31 0.7	18:12 0.3	08:44 6.3	21:20 5.8
14 Wed		10:21 3.9	23:01 3.1	04:59 1.0	17:38 0.6	00:27 2.6	12:25 2.9	06:10 0.8	18:52 0.5	09:22 6.1	21:53 5.6
15 Thu		11:00 3.7	23:37 3.0	05:35 1.1	18:14 0.9	01:06 2.5	13:07 2.7	06:46 0.9	19:30 0.8	09:58 5.9	22:23 5.4
16 Fri		11:41 3.4		06:12 1.2	18:50 1.1	01:45 2.4	13:48 2.6	07:21 1.0	20:06 1.0	10:34 5.5	22:56 5.2
17 Sat	◑	00:16 2.9	12:31 3.1	06:56 1.3	19:30 1.4	02:22 2.3	14:33 2.4	07:55 1.2	20:39 1.2	11:14 5.1	23:35 4.9
18 Sun		01:02 2.8	13:39 2.8	07:49 1.5	20:24 1.6	03:03 2.3	15:24 2.2	08:45 1.3	21:18 1.4		12:08 4.7
19 Mon		02:03 2.8	15:13 2.7	09:05 1.5	22:05 1.8	03:52 2.2	16:33 2.1	10:12 1.4	22:23 1.6	00:32 4.6	13:35 4.4
20 Tue		03:18 2.7	17:03 2.7	11:12 1.4	23:42 1.7	04:51 2.2	19:00 2.1		12:21 1.3	02:06 4.5	15:24 4.4
21 Wed		04:35 2.8	18:11 2.9		12:15 1.3	05:51 2.3	20:02 2.2	00:06 1.6	13:19 1.1	03:44 4.6	16:40 4.7
22 Thu		05:44 3.0	18:56 3.0	00:35 1.6	13:03 1.1	06:45 2.3	20:43 2.3	01:15 1.5	14:00 0.9	04:48 4.9	17:30 5.0
23 Fri		06:28 3.2	19:29 3.1	01:15 1.4	13:43 1.0	07:35 2.4	21:15 2.4	01:55 1.3	14:36 0.8	05:33 5.3	18:08 5.3
24 Sat		07:04 3.4	19:58 3.2	01:44 1.4	14:17 0.8	08:22 2.5	21:42 2.4	02:32 1.2	15:12 0.6	06:11 5.6	18:42 5.5
25 Sun	●	07:37 3.5	20:24 3.2	02:11 1.3	14:51 0.7	09:09 2.6	22:10 2.5	03:10 1.0	15:50 0.5	06:44 5.8	19:14 5.7
26 Mon		08:11 3.7	20:51 3.3	02:43 1.1	15:26 0.6	09:54 2.7	22:42 2.5	03:49 0.9	16:28 0.4	07:17 5.9	19:44 5.8
27 Tue		08:45 3.8	21:21 3.4	03:18 1.0	16:00 0.6	10:36 2.7	23:16 2.5	04:27 0.8	17:06 0.4	07:49 6.0	20:16 5.9
28 Wed		09:20 3.8	21:53 3.4	03:54 1.0	16:34 0.6	11:15 2.7	23:49 2.5	05:03 0.8	17:41 0.5	08:21 6.1	20:48 5.9
29 Thu		09:56 3.8	22:27 3.3	04:29 1.0	17:08 0.7	11:51 2.7		05:36 0.8	18:15 0.6	08:55 6.0	21:21 5.8
30 Fri		10:33 3.7	23:04 3.2	05:05 1.1	17:43 0.9	00:20 2.4	12:24 2.7	06:08 0.8	18:45 0.8	09:30 5.9	21:56 5.6

Tidal information computed by POLTIPS software developed by National Oceanography Centre

October 2022

Times: GMT / BST   Heights: metres (above chart datum)

Day	HUNSTANTON HW AM	HW PM	LW AM	LW PM	CROMER/SHERINGHAM HW AM	HW PM	LW AM	LW PM	BLAKENEY BAR HW AM	HW PM
1 Sat	10:11 6.7	22:38 6.3	04:50 1.5	17:16 1.6	10:24 4.8	22:56 4.5	04:45 1.2	17:13 1.3	10:17 5.4	22:43 5.1
2 Sun	11:05 6.2	23:31 5.8	05:27 1.8	17:55 2.0	11:21 4.5	23:51 4.3	05:29 1.4	18:01 1.6	11:08 5.0	23:36 4.8
3 Mon ◑		12:19 5.6	06:20 2.1	18:52 2.4		12:40 4.2	06:28 1.6	19:09 2.0		12:18 4.7
4 Tue	00:48 5.5	14:07 5.4	07:39 2.3	20:21 2.7	01:10 4.0	14:33 4.0	07:56 1.8	20:48 2.2	00:48 4.6	14:05 4.5
5 Wed	02:31 5.4	15:48 5.6	09:32 2.1	22:08 2.5	02:54 4.1	16:08 4.2	09:48 1.7	22:27 2.0	02:29 4.5	15:51 4.7
6 Thu	03:58 5.8	16:59 6.1	11:03 1.6	23:25 2.1	04:14 4.3	17:16 4.5	11:13 1.3	23:32 1.7	04:02 4.8	17:04 5.0
7 Fri	05:00 6.2	17:53 6.6	11:53 1.1		05:13 4.6	18:06 4.7	11:57 1.0		05:06 5.2	17:57 5.4
8 Sat	05:50 6.8	18:38 7.0	00:23 1.6	13:06 0.7	06:06 5.0	18:47 4.9	00:22 1.4	13:10 0.7	05:53 5.5	18:39 5.6
9 Sun ○	06:33 7.2	19:17 7.3	01:12 1.2	13:52 0.4	06:40 5.2	19:23 5.0	01:06 1.2	13:57 0.6	06:33 5.8	19:16 5.6
10 Mon	07:11 7.5	19:51 7.3	01:54 0.9	14:33 0.4	07:18 5.3	19:57 5.0	01:48 1.0	14:37 0.6	07:09 5.9	19:48 5.7
11 Tue	07:47 7.5	20:24 7.3	02:32 0.9	15:09 0.5	07:54 5.4	20:29 5.0	02:27 0.9	15:11 0.6	07:46 6.0	20:19 5.6
12 Wed	08:21 7.4	20:54 7.1	03:04 0.9	15:38 0.8	08:30 5.3	20:59 4.9	03:03 0.9	15:39 0.8	08:23 5.9	20:51 5.5
13 Thu	08:55 7.2	21:22 6.8	03:33 1.0	16:01 1.1	09:06 5.1	21:30 4.8	03:37 1.0	16:01 1.0	08:59 5.7	21:23 5.4
14 Fri	09:30 6.8	21:51 6.5	03:59 1.3	16:21 1.5	09:42 4.8	22:00 4.6	04:09 1.2	16:24 1.3	09:36 5.4	21:52 5.2
15 Sat	10:05 6.4	22:20 6.1	04:27 1.6	16:42 1.8	10:21 4.5	22:34 4.4	04:39 1.4	16:52 1.6	10:12 5.1	22:24 5.0
16 Sun	10:45 5.8	22:54 5.7	04:57 1.9	17:10 2.2	11:07 4.2	23:15 4.2	05:15 1.6	17:27 1.9	10:52 4.7	23:02 4.7
17 Mon ●	11:38 5.3	23:42 4.9	05:36 2.3	17:50 2.7		12:09 3.8	06:01 1.9	18:15 2.2	11:45 4.4	23:55 4.4
18 Tue		13:02 4.9	06:30 2.6	18:49 3.0	00:16 3.9	13:51 3.6	07:12 2.1	19:30 2.5		13:07 4.1
19 Wed	01:09 5.0	14:54 4.9	07:57 2.8	20:23 3.2	02:06 3.8	15:25 3.7	08:54 2.2	21:14 2.6	01:19 4.2	14:52 4.1
20 Thu	03:00 5.1	16:12 5.3	09:48 2.6	22:01 2.8	03:33 3.9	16:30 3.9	10:22 1.9	22:38 2.3	03:01 4.2	16:09 4.4
21 Fri	04:09 5.5	17:04 5.8	11:04 2.1	23:06 2.4	04:32 4.1	17:15 4.1	11:18 1.6	23:30 2.0	04:12 4.5	17:00 4.7
22 Sat	04:57 6.0	17:45 6.2	11:53 1.7	23:56 1.9	05:15 4.4	17:50 4.4		12:02 1.4	05:01 4.9	17:40 5.0
23 Sun	05:36 6.5	18:21 6.6		12:39 1.3	05:51 4.6	18:22 4.6	00:11 1.7	12:42 1.1	05:41 5.2	18:14 5.2
24 Mon	06:11 6.9	18:53 6.9	00:42 1.5	13:22 1.0	06:22 4.9	18:54 4.8	00:49 1.4	13:20 0.9	06:16 5.4	18:46 5.4
25 Tue ●	06:45 7.2	19:24 7.2	01:25 1.2	14:03 0.8	06:53 5.0	19:26 5.0	01:27 1.1	13:57 0.8	06:50 5.6	19:18 5.6
26 Wed	07:19 7.4	19:54 7.4	02:06 1.1	14:40 0.8	07:27 5.2	20:00 5.0	02:03 1.0	14:32 0.7	07:23 5.7	19:51 5.6
27 Thu	07:55 7.4	20:26 7.1	02:46 1.0	15:16 0.8	08:04 5.2	20:35 5.0	02:39 0.9	15:06 0.7	07:59 5.8	20:25 5.6
28 Fri	08:33 7.3	21:00 7.0	03:24 1.1	15:50 0.9	08:45 5.2	21:12 5.0	03:15 0.9	15:40 0.9	08:38 5.8	21:02 5.6
29 Sat	09:17 7.0	21:39 6.7	04:01 1.2	16:24 1.2	09:31 5.0	21:51 4.8	03:52 1.0	16:17 1.1	09:21 5.6	21:42 5.4
30 Sun	09:07 6.6	21:24 6.4	03:40 1.3	16:00 1.6	09:24 4.8	21:38 4.6	03:33 1.1	15:59 1.4	09:10 5.3	21:29 5.2
31 Mon										

Tidal information computed by POLTIPS software developed by National Oceanography Centre

Times: GMT / BST

October 2022

Heights: metres (above chart datum)

Day	Moon	WINTERTON HW AM	WINTERTON HW PM	WINTERTON LW AM	WINTERTON LW PM	GORLESTON HW AM	GORLESTON HW PM	GORLESTON LW AM	GORLESTON LW PM	WELLS BAR HW AM	WELLS BAR HW PM
1 Sat		11:15 3.5	23:46 3.1	05:44 1.1	18:22 1.0	00:50 2.4	13:01 2.6	06:42 0.9	19:18 0.9	10:10 5.7	22:35 5.4
2 Sun			12:10 3.3		19:11 1.3	01:25 2.4	13:52 2.5	07:24 1.0	20:03 1.2	10:59 5.4	23:26 5.1
3 Mon	◑	00:40 3.0	13:25 3.1	07:38 1.2	20:22 1.5	02:16 2.3	15:06 2.5	08:35 1.0	21:17 1.4		12:06 5.0
4 Tue		01:48 2.9	14:59 3.0	09:07 1.3	21:57 1.6	03:28 2.3	16:58 2.3	10:18 1.1	22:45 1.4	00:35 4.9	13:50 4.8
5 Wed		03:06 2.9	16:41 3.1	10:44 1.1	23:19 1.6	04:51 2.3	18:39 2.3	11:48 0.9		02:14 4.8	15:37 5.0
6 Thu		04:21 3.0	18:02 3.3		12:02 0.9	06:04 2.4	19:54 2.4	00:05 1.4	13:04 0.7	03:48 5.1	16:53 5.3
7 Fri		05:29 3.3	18:53 3.4	00:24 1.5	13:06 0.7	07:02 2.5	20:48 2.5	01:14 1.3	14:06 0.6	04:55 5.5	17:48 5.7
8 Sat		06:26 3.3	19:34 3.4	01:18 1.4	13:57 0.6	07:47 2.7	21:29 2.6	02:12 1.1	14:57 0.4	05:44 5.8	18:32 5.8
9 Sun	○	07:13 3.8	20:10 3.5	02:04 1.2	14:41 0.5	08:47 2.7	22:06 2.6	03:00 1.0	15:42 0.3	06:26 6.0	19:10 5.9
10 Mon		07:56 3.9	20:45 3.5	02:44 1.1	15:20 0.4	09:40 2.8	22:42 2.6	03:44 0.8	16:24 0.3	07:03 6.2	19:43 6.0
11 Tue		08:38 4.0	21:20 3.4	03:21 1.0	15:56 0.5	10:30 2.8	23:19 2.6	04:26 0.7	17:04 0.4	07:41 6.2	20:14 5.9
12 Wed		09:19 3.9	21:54 3.4	03:58 1.0	16:31 0.7	11:17 2.8	23:57 2.6	05:06 0.7	17:42 0.5	08:18 6.2	20:46 5.8
13 Thu		09:58 3.7	22:27 3.3	04:34 1.0	17:04 0.9		12:00 2.7	05:45 0.8	18:18 0.7	08:54 6.0	21:17 5.7
14 Fri		10:38 3.4	22:58 3.2	05:10 1.1	17:35 1.1	00:32 2.5	12:39 2.6	06:19 0.9	18:47 1.0	09:30 5.7	21:46 5.5
15 Sat		11:19 3.2	23:32 3.1	05:47 1.2	18:05 1.3	01:02 2.4	13:14 2.4	06:45 1.0	18:58 1.2	10:05 5.4	22:17 5.3
16 Sun			12:10 2.9	06:28 1.2	18:41 1.5	01:20 2.4	13:50 2.2	07:10 1.1	19:14 1.3	10:44 5.0	22:53 5.0
17 Mon	◐	00:12 3.0	13:17 2.7	07:19 1.4	19:28 1.7	01:43 2.4	14:41 2.1	07:57 1.2	19:57 1.5	11:34 4.7	23:44 4.7
18 Tue		01:07 2.9	14:44 2.6	08:26 1.4	20:44 1.9	02:45 2.3	15:49 2.0	09:12 1.3	21:03 1.6		12:53 4.4
19 Wed		02:17 2.8	16:12 2.7	10:18 1.4	23:03 1.9	03:54 2.2	17:24 2.0	11:05 1.2	22:34 1.6	01:05 4.5	14:37 4.4
20 Thu		03:33 2.8	17:28 2.8	11:29 1.2	23:53 1.7	05:03 2.2	19:17 2.2		12:17 1.1	02:46 4.6	15:56 4.6
21 Fri		04:40 2.9	18:15 3.0		12:17 1.1	06:06 2.3	19:53 2.3	00:11 1.5	13:04 0.9	03:59 4.8	16:49 5.0
22 Sat		05:34 3.1	18:48 3.1	00:29 1.6	12:58 1.0	07:03 2.4	20:22 2.4	01:09 1.3	13:48 0.7	04:50 5.2	17:30 5.3
23 Sun		06:18 3.3	19:17 3.2	00:59 1.4	13:35 0.9	07:53 2.5	20:56 2.5	01:55 1.2	14:30 0.6	05:32 5.5	18:06 5.5
24 Mon		06:58 3.5	19:46 3.3	01:34 1.3	14:11 0.7	08:40 2.6	21:33 2.5	02:39 1.0	15:12 0.5	06:08 5.7	18:39 5.7
25 Tue	●	07:37 3.7	20:16 3.4	02:11 1.1	14:48 0.6	09:25 2.6	22:09 2.5	03:21 0.9	15:54 0.4	06:43 5.9	19:12 5.9
26 Wed		08:16 3.8	20:50 3.5	02:52 1.0	15:26 0.6	10:08 2.7	22:46 2.5	04:01 0.8	16:33 0.4	07:17 6.0	19:46 5.9
27 Thu		08:54 3.8	21:25 3.5	03:32 1.0	16:03 0.7	10:48 2.7	23:20 2.5	04:39 0.8	17:09 0.5	07:54 6.1	20:20 6.0
28 Fri		09:35 3.8	22:02 3.5	04:13 0.9	16:41 0.8	11:26 2.7	23:51 2.5	05:15 0.8	17:43 0.7	08:33 6.0	20:57 5.9
29 Sat		10:20 3.6	22:41 3.4	04:55 0.9	17:20 1.0		12:06 2.6	05:51 0.8	18:15 0.8	09:15 5.9	21:36 5.7
30 Sun		10:11 3.4	22:26 3.2	04:42 1.0	17:04 1.2	00:23 2.5	*11:54 2.5	05:33 0.8	17:53 1.1	09:03 5.6	21:21 5.5
31 Mon		11:14 3.2	23:20 3.1	05:38 1.0	17:59 1.4	00:02 2.5	12:59 2.4	06:32 0.9	18:45 1.3	10:00 5.3	22:15 5.2

Tidal information computed by POLTIPS software developed by National Oceanography Centre

November 2022

Times: GMT / BST

Heights: metres (above chart datum)

Day		HUNSTANTON HW AM	HW PM	LW AM	LW PM	CROMER/SHERINGHAM HW AM	HW PM	LW AM	LW PM	BLAKENEY BAR HW AM	HW PM
1 Tue	○	11:30 5.6	23:38 5.6	05:24 1.8	17:42 2.4	11:54 4.2	23:59 4.2	05:33 1.5	18:03 2.1	11:28 4.7	23:38 4.7
2 Wed			13:06 5.5	06:48 1.9	19:10 2.6		13:33 4.1	07:09 1.6	19:36 2.2		13:15 4.6
3 Thu		01:12 5.6	14:30 5.7	08:25 1.7	20:47 2.5	01:34 4.2	14:56 4.2	08:45 1.4	21:03 2.0	01:13 4.7	14:39 4.8
4 Fri		02:33 5.9	15:36 6.1	09:42 1.4	21:58 2.1	02:49 4.4	15:58 4.4	09:57 1.2	22:05 1.8	02:38 4.9	15:44 5.0
5 Sat		03:33 6.4	16:27 6.5	10:44 1.0	22:54 1.7	03:48 4.7	16:45 4.6	10:54 1.0	22:55 1.5	03:40 5.2	16:34 5.3
6 Sun		04:24 6.8	17:09 6.8	11:36 0.8	23:41 1.3	04:35 4.9	17:23 4.8	11:42 0.8	23:39 1.3	04:27 5.4	17:14 5.4
7 Mon		05:07 7.1	17:48 7.0		12:20 0.7	05:16 5.0	17:56 4.8		12:24 0.8	05:07 5.6	17:48 5.5
8 Tue	○	05:46 7.2	18:22 7.1	00:22 1.1	12:59 0.8	05:54 5.1	18:28 4.9	00:21 1.1	12:59 0.8	05:45 5.7	18:19 5.5
9 Wed		06:24 7.2	18:54 7.0	01:00 1.1	13:31 0.9	06:33 5.1	18:59 4.9	01:01 1.0	13:30 0.9	06:23 5.7	18:49 5.5
10 Thu		06:59 7.0	19:23 6.9	01:33 1.1	13:57 1.2	07:09 5.0	19:29 4.9	01:39 1.0	13:57 1.0	07:00 5.6	19:21 5.5
11 Fri		07:33 6.8	19:51 6.7	02:02 1.2	14:18 1.4	07:47 4.8	20:00 4.8	02:13 1.1	14:24 1.2	07:37 5.5	19:52 5.4
12 Sat		08:08 6.5	20:19 6.5	02:30 1.4	14:39 1.6	08:24 4.6	20:30 4.7	02:45 1.2	14:51 1.4	08:14 5.2	20:23 5.2
13 Sun		08:45 6.2	20:48 6.2	02:57 1.6	15:06 1.8	09:04 4.4	21:03 4.5	03:17 1.3	15:23 1.6	08:51 5.0	20:55 5.1
14 Mon		09:26 5.8	21:21 5.9	03:30 1.8	15:37 2.1	09:48 4.1	21:42 4.3	03:53 1.5	15:59 1.9	09:31 4.7	21:33 4.8
15 Tue		10:16 5.5	22:06 5.5	04:08 2.1	16:18 2.4	10:41 3.9	22:32 4.1	04:37 1.7	16:43 2.1	10:19 4.4	22:21 4.6
16 Wed	●	11:23 5.1	23:12 5.2	04:58 2.3	17:12 2.7	11:53 3.7	23:51 3.9	05:38 1.9	17:42 2.4	11:23 4.2	23:26 4.4
17 Thu			12:48 5.0	06:09 2.5	18:27 2.9		13:18 3.7	06:58 2.0	19:04 2.5		12:47 4.2
18 Fri		00:43 5.2	14:30 5.2	07:41 2.4	19:57 2.8	01:24 3.9	14:30 3.8	08:11 1.9	20:29 2.3	00:50 4.3	14:04 4.3
19 Sat		02:03 5.4	15:09 5.5	09:03 2.1	21:12 2.4	02:32 4.0	15:24 4.0	09:21 1.7	21:36 2.1	02:08 4.5	15:04 4.6
20 Sun		03:02 5.9	15:56 6.0	10:03 1.8	22:11 2.0	03:22 4.3	16:06 4.3	10:13 1.4	22:27 1.8	03:06 4.8	15:52 4.8
21 Mon		03:48 6.3	16:36 6.3	10:54 1.4	23:01 1.7	04:03 4.5	16:43 4.5	10:59 1.2	23:12 1.5	03:54 5.0	16:33 5.1
22 Tue		04:30 6.7	17:13 6.6	11:40 1.2	23:48 1.4	04:41 4.7	17:18 4.7	11:41 1.0	23:54 1.3	04:36 5.3	17:11 5.3
23 Wed	●	05:12 7.0	17:49 6.9		12:24 1.0	05:21 4.9	17:54 4.9		12:22 0.9	05:16 5.5	17:48 5.5
24 Thu		05:54 7.2	18:26 7.0	00:35 1.2	13:07 0.9	06:03 5.1	18:33 5.0	00:35 1.1	13:03 0.8	05:56 5.6	18:26 5.6
25 Fri		06:39 7.2	19:04 7.0	01:21 1.1	13:48 0.8	06:49 5.1	19:12 5.1	01:16 0.9	13:43 0.8	06:40 5.7	19:04 5.7
26 Sat		07:26 7.1	19:45 7.0	02:06 1.0	14:28 0.9	07:39 5.1	19:54 5.0	02:00 0.9	14:24 0.9	07:27 5.7	19:46 5.6
27 Sun		08:18 6.9	20:28 6.8	02:51 1.0	15:08 1.1	08:32 5.0	20:39 4.9	02:45 0.9	15:07 1.1	08:16 5.6	20:32 5.5
28 Mon		09:13 6.6	21:16 6.5	03:39 1.0	15:50 1.5	09:28 4.7	21:29 4.8	03:35 1.0	15:54 1.4	09:11 5.3	21:21 5.3
29 Tue		10:15 6.2	22:12 6.2	04:30 1.2	16:36 1.8	10:32 4.5	22:27 4.6	04:33 1.1	16:47 1.7	10:14 5.1	22:17 5.1
30 Wed	○	11:24 5.8	23:21 6.0	05:30 1.3	17:33 2.2	11:47 4.2	23:39 4.4	05:45 1.2	17:51 1.9	11:29 4.8	23:21 5.0

November 2022

Times: GMT / BST

Day	Moon	WINTERTON HW AM	WINTERTON HW PM	WINTERTON LW AM	WINTERTON LW PM	GORLESTON HW AM	GORLESTON HW PM	GORLESTON LW AM	GORLESTON LW PM	WELLS BAR HW AM	WELLS BAR HW PM
1 Tue	◑		12:32 3.1	06:44 1.1	19:11 1.6	01:00 2.4	14:22 2.3	07:53 0.9	20:04 1.4	11:16 5.0	23:25 5.0
2 Wed		00:25 3.0	14:08 3.0	08:06 1.0	20:40 1.7	02:15 2.4	16:00 2.3	09:12 0.9	21:23 1.5		13:00 4.9
3 Thu		01:37 3.0	15:37 3.2	09:29 0.9	21:56 1.6	03:30 2.4	17:24 2.4	10:30 0.8	22:37 1.4	00:58 5.0	14:25 5.1
4 Fri		02:51 3.1	16:44 3.2	10:40 0.8	22:58 1.5	04:39 2.5	18:30 2.4	11:39 0.6	23:44 1.3	02:24 5.2	15:32 5.4
5 Sat		04:01 3.3	17:31 3.3	11:41 0.7	23:51 1.4	05:39 2.6	19:20 2.5		12:39 0.5	03:28 5.5	16:24 5.6
6 Sun		04:59 3.5	18:10 3.3		12:31 0.7	06:34 2.6	20:01 2.5	00:42 1.1	13:30 0.5	04:17 5.7	17:06 5.7
7 Mon		05:48 3.6	18:45 3.4	00:37 1.3	13:13 0.7	07:27 2.7	20:38 2.5	01:32 1.0	14:15 0.5	04:59 5.9	17:41 5.9
8 Tue	○	06:34 3.7	19:19 3.4	01:18 1.1	13:51 0.7	08:18 2.7	21:15 2.5	02:19 0.8	14:56 0.5	05:38 6.0	18:13 5.8
9 Wed		07:18 3.7	19:52 3.4	01:58 1.0	14:26 0.8	09:08 2.7	21:51 2.6	03:03 0.8	15:35 0.6	06:17 6.0	18:44 5.8
10 Thu		08:00 3.6	20:25 3.4	02:37 1.0	14:59 0.9	09:54 2.6	22:25 2.5	03:45 0.8	16:10 0.8	06:55 5.9	19:16 5.8
11 Fri		08:42 3.4	20:55 3.4	03:14 1.0	15:29 1.1	10:33 2.5	22:51 2.5	04:23 0.8	16:36 0.9	07:32 5.8	19:47 5.7
12 Sat		09:22 3.2	21:24 3.3	03:50 1.0	15:56 1.2	11:03 2.4	23:08 2.5	04:54 0.9	16:40 1.1	08:09 5.6	20:17 5.6
13 Sun		10:04 3.0	21:53 3.2	04:28 1.1	16:21 1.4	11:16 2.3	23:54 2.5	05:12 1.0	16:59 1.2	08:45 5.3	20:49 5.4
14 Mon		10:53 2.8	22:33 3.1	05:08 1.2	16:53 1.5	11:54 2.2		05:42 1.0	17:36 1.3	09:23 5.0	21:25 5.1
15 Tue		11:50 2.7	23:23 3.0	05:56 1.3	17:38 1.7		12:51 2.1	06:30 1.1	18:23 1.4	10:09 4.7	22:11 4.9
16 Wed	◐		13:00 2.6	06:53 1.3	18:41 1.8	00:54 2.4	14:02 2.2	07:37 1.1	19:25 1.5	11:11 4.5	23:14 4.7
17 Thu		00:23 2.9	14:14 2.7	08:02 1.3	20:05 1.9	02:11 2.3	15:18 2.0	08:54 1.1	20:45 1.5		12:32 4.5
18 Fri		01:33 2.9	15:17 2.8	09:16 1.2	21:29 1.8	03:22 2.3	16:38 2.1	10:11 1.0	22:11 1.5	00:35 4.6	13:49 4.6
19 Sat		02:43 2.9	16:10 2.9	10:14 1.1	22:26 1.6	04:29 2.3	17:42 2.2	11:12 0.9	23:22 1.3	01:53 4.8	14:50 4.9
20 Sun		03:41 3.1	16:54 3.0	11:01 1.0	23:11 1.5	05:29 2.4	18:33 2.3		12:05 0.7	02:53 5.0	15:40 5.2
21 Mon		04:32 3.2	17:31 3.2	11:45 0.9	23:56 1.3	06:22 2.4	19:17 2.4	00:17 1.2	12:52 0.6	03:42 5.3	16:23 5.4
22 Tue		05:04 3.4	18:08 3.3		12:29 0.8	07:10 2.5	19:59 2.5	01:06 1.0	13:38 0.5	04:26 5.6	17:03 5.6
23 Wed	●	06:04 3.5	18:45 3.4	00:41 1.2	13:12 0.7	07:56 2.6	20:39 2.5	01:51 0.9	14:21 0.5	05:08 5.8	17:41 5.8
24 Thu		06:49 3.6	19:23 3.5	01:28 1.0	13:55 0.7	08:40 2.6	21:18 2.5	02:36 0.8	15:03 0.5	05:50 6.0	18:20 5.9
25 Fri		07:35 3.7	20:02 3.6	02:15 0.9	14:38 0.8	09:24 2.7	21:54 2.6	03:19 0.8	15:42 0.6	06:35 6.0	18:59 6.0
26 Sat		08:24 3.6	20:44 3.5	03:03 0.8	15:21 0.9	10:11 2.6	22:30 2.6	04:03 0.7	16:19 0.8	07:22 6.0	19:41 5.9
27 Sun		09:18 3.5	21:27 3.5	03:53 0.8	16:06 1.1	11:03 2.6	23:08 2.6	04:52 0.7	16:58 0.9	08:11 5.8	20:26 5.8
28 Mon		10:14 3.4	22:14 3.4	04:45 0.8	16:55 1.3	*12:04 2.5	23:56 2.6	05:48 0.7	17:44 1.1	09:05 5.6	21:14 5.6
29 Tue		11:15 3.2	23:06 3.3	05:41 0.8	17:50 1.5		13:11 2.4	06:48 0.7	18:43 1.3	10:05 5.4	22:08 5.4
30 Wed	◑	12:27 3.0		06:42 0.8	18:53 1.6	00:59 2.6	14:21 2.3	07:51 0.7	19:49 1.4	11:17 5.1	23:09 5.3

Tidal information computed by POLTIPS software developed by National Oceanography Centre

December 2022

Times: GMT / BST

Heights: metres (above chart datum)

Day	HUNSTANTON				CROMER/SHERINGHAM				BLAKENEY BAR	
	HW AM	HW PM	LW AM	LW PM	HW AM	HW PM	LW AM	LW PM	HW AM	HW PM
1 Thu		12:40 5.7	06:40 1.4	18:45 2.4		13:08 4.1	07:04 1.3	19:05 2.0		12:57 4.7
2 Fri	00:39 5.9	13:54 5.7	07:55 1.4	20:05 2.3	01:00 4.4	14:23 4.2	08:19 1.3	20:21 2.0	00:40 4.9	14:09 4.8
3 Sat	01:55 6.0	14:58 5.9	09:06 1.3	21:16 2.1	02:12 4.4	15:25 4.2	09:24 1.2	21:27 1.8	02:00 4.9	15:09 4.9
4 Sun	03:00 6.2	15:52 6.2	10:07 1.2	22:15 1.8	03:14 4.6	16:15 4.4	10:20 1.2	22:22 1.6	03:05 5.0	16:01 5.0
5 Mon	03:54 6.5	16:38 6.4	10:59 1.2	23:06 1.5	04:06 4.7	16:54 4.5	11:08 1.1	23:12 1.4	03:58 5.1	16:44 5.1
6 Tue	04:42 6.6	17:19 6.6	11:43 1.2	23:51 1.4	04:53 4.7	17:30 4.6	11:48 1.1	23:57 1.3	04:43 5.3	17:20 5.2
7 Wed	05:26 6.7	17:57 6.7		12:21 1.3	05:36 4.8	18:03 4.7		12:24 1.2	05:25 5.3	17:54 5.3
8 Thu ○	06:06 6.6	18:28 6.7	00:30 1.3	12:51 1.4	06:17 4.8	18:36 4.8	00:40 1.2	12:57 1.2	06:05 5.4	18:26 5.4
9 Fri	06:44 6.5	18:59 6.6	01:06 1.4	13:18 1.4	06:56 4.7	19:08 4.8	01:20 1.1	13:28 1.2	06:44 5.3	18:58 5.4
10 Sat	07:22 6.4	19:29 6.6	01:38 1.4	13:43 1.5	07:35 4.6	19:40 4.8	01:57 1.1	14:00 1.3	07:22 5.2	19:31 5.4
11 Sun	07:57 6.3	19:58 6.4	02:09 1.5	14:12 1.6	08:12 4.5	20:12 4.7	02:30 1.2	14:31 1.4	07:59 5.1	20:04 5.3
12 Mon	08:35 6.2	20:28 6.3	02:40 1.5	14:43 1.6	08:51 4.4	20:45 4.6	03:04 1.3	15:05 1.5	08:36 5.0	20:38 5.2
13 Tue	09:15 6.0	21:03 6.1	03:15 1.6	15:18 1.8	09:30 4.2	21:20 4.5	03:39 1.4	15:41 1.7	09:14 4.8	21:15 5.0
14 Wed	09:58 5.7	21:43 5.9	03:53 1.7	15:58 2.0	10:13 4.1	22:01 4.3	04:20 1.5	16:20 1.9	09:56 4.6	21:56 4.8
15 Thu	10:49 5.5	22:35 5.7	04:39 1.9	16:45 2.3	11:03 3.9	22:52 4.2	05:08 1.6	17:06 2.0	10:44 4.5	22:46 4.7
16 Fri ●	11:48 5.3	23:40 5.5	05:34 2.0	17:42 2.5	*12:03 3.8	23:57 4.1	06:06 1.7	18:03 2.2	11:42 4.4	23:44 4.6
17 Sat		12:55 5.3	06:39 2.1	18:50 2.6		13:09 3.8	07:09 1.7	19:12 2.2		12:50 4.4
18 Sun	00:52 5.6	14:00 5.3	07:50 2.1	20:03 2.4	01:06 4.1	14:14 3.9	08:14 1.7	20:24 2.1	00:53 4.6	13:58 4.5
19 Mon	02:00 5.8	14:57 5.6	09:00 1.9	21:13 2.2	02:11 4.1	15:11 4.1	09:16 1.5	21:31 1.9	02:03 4.7	14:57 4.7
20 Tue	02:59 6.1	15:48 5.9	10:02 1.7	22:15 1.9	03:09 4.3	16:00 4.3	10:13 1.3	22:30 1.6	03:04 4.9	15:50 4.9
21 Wed	03:54 6.4	16:36 6.3	10:57 1.5	23:13 1.6	04:04 4.6	16:45 4.6	11:06 1.2	23:22 1.4	03:57 5.1	16:39 5.2
22 Thu	04:48 6.6	17:21 6.6	11:49 1.2		04:57 4.8	17:30 4.8	11:54 1.0		04:50 5.3	17:25 5.4
23 Fri ●	05:41 6.8	18:06 6.8	00:09 1.4	12:39 1.0	05:51 4.9	18:13 4.9	00:12 1.1	12:42 0.9	05:42 5.5	18:08 5.5
24 Sat	06:35 7.0	18:51 7.0	01:05 1.1	13:28 0.9	06:44 5.0	18:58 5.0	01:03 0.9	13:29 0.9	06:33 5.6	18:52 5.6
25 Sun	07:28 7.0	19:36 7.0	02:00 0.8	14:15 0.9	07:37 5.0	19:44 5.1	01:55 0.8	14:15 1.0	07:25 5.6	19:37 5.7
26 Mon	08:21 6.9	20:21 7.0	02:52 0.7	15:01 1.0	08:30 5.1	20:30 5.1	02:50 0.7	15:02 1.1	08:16 5.6	20:24 5.7
27 Tue	09:14 6.8	21:08 6.8	03:42 0.6	15:45 1.2	09:25 4.8	21:19 5.0	03:47 0.8	15:48 1.2	09:10 5.4	21:12 5.6
28 Wed	10:08 6.5	21:58 6.6	04:33 0.6	16:30 1.5	10:21 4.6	22:09 4.7	04:44 0.8	16:35 1.4	10:06 5.2	22:02 5.4
29 Thu	11:02 6.1	22:55 6.3	05:23 0.8	17:17 1.8	11:20 4.4	23:09 4.7	05:40 0.9	17:26 1.6	11:08 5.0	22:56 5.2
30 Fri ○	12:01 5.8		06:16 1.0	18:10 2.0	12:24 4.1		06:36 1.1	18:23 1.8	*12:16 4.8	23:57 5.0

Tidal information computed by POLTIPS software developed by National Oceanography Centre

December 2022

Heights: metres (above chart datum)

Day	WINTERTON HW AM	WINTERTON HW PM	WINTERTON LW AM	WINTERTON LW PM	GORLESTON HW AM	GORLESTON HW PM	GORLESTON LW AM	GORLESTON LW PM	WELLS BAR HW AM	WELLS BAR HW PM
1 Thu	00:03 3.2	13:53 3.0	07:50 0.8	20:05 1.7	02:04 2.5	15:36 2.3	08:56 0.7	20:54 1.4	00:26 5.2	12:42 5.0
2 Fri	01:06 3.2	15:10 3.0	09:00 0.8	21:17 1.7	03:09 2.5	16:51 2.3	10:03 0.7	22:02 1.4	01:45 5.2	13:54 5.1
3 Sat	02:18 3.2	16:12 3.0	10:08 0.8	22:21 1.6	04:14 2.6	17:54 2.3	11:09 0.6	23:09 1.3	02:51 5.4	14:56 5.2
4 Sun	03:28 3.2	17:02 3.1	11:08 0.8	23:19 1.4	05:17 2.6	18:48 2.4		12:09 0.6	03:47 5.5	15:50 5.3
5 Mon	04:32 3.3	17:44 3.2		12:00 0.9	06:15 2.6	19:33 2.4	00:11 1.2	13:02 0.7	04:34 5.6	16:35 5.4
6 Tue	05:29 3.3	18:22 3.2	00:11 1.3	12:44 0.9	07:09 2.6	20:14 2.4	01:09 0.9	13:48 0.7	05:17 5.6	17:12 5.5
7 Wed	06:20 3.4	18:56 3.3	00:57 1.1	13:23 1.0	08:03 2.5	20:51 2.5	02:01 0.9	14:30 0.8	05:59 5.7	17:47 5.6
8 Thu ○	07:07 3.3	19:30 3.4	01:41 1.0	13:58 1.0	08:53 2.5	21:26 2.5	02:48 0.9	15:06 0.8	06:39 5.7	18:20 5.7
9 Fri	07:52 3.2	20:01 3.4	02:22 1.0	14:31 1.1	09:38 2.4	21:50 2.5	03:32 0.8	15:33 1.0	07:17 5.6	18:53 5.7
10 Sat	08:34 3.1	20:30 3.4	03:01 1.0	14:59 1.2	10:12 2.3	21:34 2.6	04:09 0.8	15:39 1.0	07:54 5.4	19:26 5.7
11 Sun	09:13 3.0	20:58 3.4	03:38 1.0	15:22 1.3	10:07 2.3	22:04 2.6	04:39 0.9	16:00 1.1	08:30 5.3	19:59 5.6
12 Mon	09:52 2.9	21:30 3.3	04:16 1.0	15:47 1.4	10:40 2.3	22:45 2.6	05:00 0.9	16:35 1.1	09:07 5.1	20:32 5.5
13 Tue	10:33 2.8	22:09 3.3	04:54 1.0	16:22 1.4	11:26 2.2	23:33 2.6	05:35 0.9	17:17 1.1	09:47 4.9	21:08 5.3
14 Wed	11:17 2.7	22:52 3.2	05:35 1.0	17:05 1.5		12:21 2.2	06:23 0.9	18:04 1.2	10:33 4.8	21:47 5.2
15 Thu	*12:07 2.6	23:41 3.1	06:22 1.1	17:58 1.6	00:31 2.5	13:24 2.1	07:18 0.9	19:00 1.3	11:29 4.7	22:35 5.0
16 Fri		13:07 2.6	07:14 1.1	19:01 1.7	01:38 2.4	14:32 2.1	08:16 1.0	20:06 1.4		23:31 4.9
17 Sat	00:35 3.0	14:12 2.6	08:11 1.1	20:14 1.7	02:42 2.3	15:45 2.1	09:20 0.9	21:18 1.4	00:38 4.9	12:35 4.6
18 Sun	01:40 3.0	15:10 2.8	09:12 1.1	21:26 1.6	03:47 2.3	16:57 2.1	10:26 0.9	22:35 1.3	01:48 5.0	13:43 4.8
19 Mon	02:50 3.1	16:02 2.9	10:11 1.0	22:29 1.5	04:51 2.3	17:55 2.2	11:26 0.8	23:40 1.2	02:50 5.2	14:43 5.0
20 Tue	03:50 3.1	16:50 3.0	11:04 0.9	23:23 1.3	05:50 2.4	18:45 2.3		12:18 0.7	03:46 5.4	15:38 5.2
21 Wed	04:45 3.2	17:35 3.2	11:54 0.9		06:42 2.5	19:30 2.4	00:36 1.1	13:07 0.6	04:41 5.6	16:29 5.4
22 Thu	05:37 3.4	18:19 3.4	00:17 1.2	12:43 0.8	07:31 2.6	20:12 2.5	01:27 1.0	13:53 0.6	05:35 5.8	17:17 5.7
23 Fri ●	06:31 3.5	19:02 3.4	01:11 1.0	13:32 0.9	08:21 2.6	20:53 2.5	02:18 0.8	14:37 0.6	06:27 6.0	18:02 5.8
24 Sat	07:28 3.5	19:46 3.5	02:05 0.8	14:21 0.9	09:13 2.6	21:33 2.6	03:10 0.7	15:21 0.7	07:20 5.9	18:47 6.0
25 Sun	08:24 3.5	20:32 3.6	02:59 0.7	15:10 1.0	10:12 2.6	22:16 2.7	04:05 0.6	16:06 0.8	08:11 6.0	19:32 6.0
26 Mon	09:18 3.5	21:16 3.6	03:51 0.5	15:58 1.1	11:12 2.6	23:04 2.7	04:58 0.5	16:54 0.9	09:03 5.9	20:18 6.0
27 Tue	10:10 3.3	22:01 3.6	04:42 0.5	16:45 1.2	*12:09 2.5	23:57 2.7	05:51 0.4	17:43 1.0	09:57 5.5	21:05 5.9
28 Wed	11:03 3.2	22:48 3.6	05:33 0.5	17:33 1.3		13:03 2.4	06:42 0.4	18:33 1.1	10:56 5.3	21:53 5.7
29 Thu	*12:02 3.0	23:38 3.5	06:26 0.6	18:24 1.5	00:51 2.7	13:59 2.3	07:35 0.5	19:25 1.2	*12:02 5.1	22:45 5.6
30 Fri		13:15 2.8	07:21 0.7	19:20 1.6	01:45 2.7	15:01 2.2	08:30 0.6	20:21 1.3		23:44 5.4
31 Sat	00:33 3.3	14:28 3.3	08:22 0.8	20:26 1.6	02:42 2.6	16:10 2.2	09:31 0.7	21:22 1.3		13:07 5.0

Tidal information computed by POLTIPS software developed by National Oceanography Centre

Tidal Site Data

Site	Blakeney Bar	Cromer	Gorleston	Hun-stanton	Wells Bar	Winter-ton
Latitude	52°59' N	52°56' N	52°34' N	52°56' N	52°59' N	52°43' N
Longitude	0°59' E	1°18' E	1°44' E	0°29' E	0°49' E	1°42' E
Ordnance Datum Offset	N/A	-2.75	-1.56	-3.75	N/A	-1.82
Highest Astronomical Tide	6.25	5.66	3.05	7.96	6.55	4.30
Lowest Astronomical Tide	N/A	0.14	0	-0.25	N/A	0.11
Mean High Water Springs	5.70	5.03	2.65	6.85	6.00	3.20
Mean High Water Neaps	4.50	3.96	2.18	5.31	4.80	2.60
Mean Low Water Neaps	N/A	1.89	1.18	2.29	N/A	1.20
Mean Low Water Springs	N/A	0.82	0.71	0.74	N/A	0.60
Average Flood	N/A	05:43	06:15	05:40	N/A	05:31
Average Ebb	N/A	06:41	06:09	06:44	N/A	06:53

January 2022

Times: GMT / BST

Heights: metres (above chart datum)

Day			HUNSTANTON				CROMER/SHERINGHAM				BLAKENEY BAR	
			HW AM	HW PM	LW AM	LW PM	HW AM	HW PM	LW AM	LW PM	HW AM	HW PM
1	Sat		04:26 6.7	17:03 6.6	11:26 1.2	23:49 1.3	04:39 4.8	17:15 4.7	11:33 1.0	23:53 1.1	04:27 5.4	17:05 5.3
2	Sun	●	05:27 6.9	17:54 6.8		12:23 1.0	05:39 5.0	18:02 4.9		12:27 0.9	05:27 5.5	17:54 5.5
3	Mon		06:24 7.0	18:41 7.0	00:51 1.0	13:16 0.9	06:33 5.1	18:47 5.1	00:51 0.9	13:17 0.9	06:22 5.6	18:39 5.7
4	Tue		07:19 7.1	19:27 7.1	01:49 0.7	14:05 0.9	07:27 5.1	19:32 5.1	01:49 0.7	14:05 0.9	07:13 5.7	19:24 5.7
5	Wed		08:10 7.0	20:09 7.0	02:42 0.5	14:50 1.0	08:17 5.0	20:15 5.1	02:47 0.6	14:50 1.0	08:04 5.6	20:08 5.7
6	Thu		08:59 6.8	20:52 6.9	03:31 0.6	15:30 1.2	09:06 4.8	20:59 5.0	03:42 0.6	15:32 1.2	08:54 5.4	20:53 5.6
7	Fri		09:45 6.5	21:36 6.6	04:17 0.6	16:07 1.5	09:55 4.6	21:45 4.9	04:31 0.7	16:13 1.4	09:44 5.2	21:38 5.5
8	Sat		10:32 6.1	22:23 6.3	05:00 0.9	16:44 1.7	10:44 4.3	22:34 4.7	05:17 0.9	16:56 1.6	10:34 5.0	22:25 5.2
9	Sun	◐	11:21 5.7	23:17 6.0	05:43 1.2	17:26 2.0	11:38 4.1	23:30 4.5	06:03 1.2	17:43 1.8	11:27 4.7	23:16 5.0
10	Mon			12:17 5.4	06:30 1.6	18:18 2.2		12:39 3.9	06:51 1.4	18:39 2.0		12:28 4.5
11	Tue		00:21 5.7	13:21 5.3	07:24 1.9	19:23 2.4	00:37 4.3	13:45 3.8	07:46 1.6	19:47 2.1	00:16 4.8	13:32 4.4
12	Wed		01:33 5.5	14:28 5.3	08:26 2.1	20:38 2.4	01:51 4.1	14:51 3.8	08:49 1.8	21:03 2.1	01:29 4.6	14:37 4.4
13	Thu		02:44 5.5	15:29 5.5	09:27 2.1	21:45 2.2	03:01 4.1	15:48 4.0	09:51 1.8	22:12 1.9	02:43 4.5	15:35 4.5
14	Fri		03:45 5.6	16:20 5.8	10:18 2.2	22:39 2.0	04:03 4.1	16:35 4.2	10:42 1.7	23:06 1.7	03:50 4.6	16:24 4.7
15	Sat		04:38 5.8	17:03 6.0	11:01 1.8	23:27 1.8	04:54 4.2	17:16 4.4	11:26 1.6	23:53 1.5	04:42 4.8	17:06 4.9
16	Sun		05:24 6.0	17:41 6.2	11:42 1.7		05:38 4.3	17:53 4.5		12:05 1.5	05:27 4.9	17:43 5.1
17	Mon	○	06:07 6.2	18:15 6.4	00:12 1.6	12:21 1.5	06:17 4.4	18:27 4.6	00:35 1.3	12:42 1.4	06:05 5.0	18:17 5.2
18	Tue		06:47 6.4	18:48 6.5	00:56 1.4	13:03 1.4	06:53 4.5	19:00 4.7	01:14 1.2	13:18 1.3	06:40 5.1	18:50 5.3
19	Wed		07:25 6.4	19:19 6.6	01:40 1.3	13:42 1.3	07:27 4.6	19:31 4.8	01:51 1.1	13:53 1.2	07:16 5.2	19:23 5.4
20	Thu		08:01 6.5	19:50 6.6	02:23 1.1	14:22 1.2	08:03 4.6	20:02 4.8	02:28 1.0	14:27 1.2	07:49 5.2	19:56 5.4
21	Fri		08:36 6.5	20:22 6.6	03:03 1.1	15:00 1.3	08:39 4.6	20:33 4.8	03:04 1.0	15:02 1.2	08:26 5.2	20:31 5.4
22	Sat		09:11 6.4	20:57 6.6	03:42 1.1	15:35 1.4	09:17 4.6	21:07 4.8	03:39 1.0	15:36 1.3	09:03 5.2	21:06 5.4
23	Sun		09:47 6.2	21:38 6.5	04:17 1.2	16:09 1.6	09:57 4.4	21:46 4.8	04:14 1.0	16:11 1.4	09:41 5.1	21:44 5.3
24	Mon		10:27 6.0	22:25 6.1	04:51 1.3	16:45 1.7	10:40 4.3	22:32 4.7	04:51 1.1	16:51 1.5	10:23 4.9	22:27 5.2
25	Tue	●	11:16 5.7	23:22 6.1	05:28 1.5	17:29 1.9	11:30 4.2	23:28 4.5	05:35 1.2	17:39 1.7	11:11 4.8	23:19 5.0
26	Wed			12:16 5.6	06:15 1.7	18:25 2.1		12:30 4.1	06:30 1.4	18:42 1.8		12:12 4.6
27	Thu		00:30 5.9	13:27 5.5	07:18 1.8	19:39 2.2	00:36 4.4	13:41 4.0	07:37 1.5	19:57 1.8	00:25 4.9	13:26 4.6
28	Fri		01:49 5.9	14:42 5.6	08:38 1.8	21:08 2.0	01:59 4.3	14:57 4.1	08:57 1.5	21:22 1.7	01:46 4.8	14:43 4.6
29	Sat		03:11 6.0	15:52 5.9	10:00 1.7	22:33 1.7	03:26 4.4	16:06 4.3	10:17 1.4	22:41 1.4	03:08 4.9	15:55 4.9
30	Sun		04:25 6.2	16:53 6.3	11:10 1.4	23:48 1.3	04:39 4.6	17:03 4.6	11:21 1.3	23:49 1.1	04:26 5.1	16:55 5.1

Tidal information computed by POLTIPS software developed by National Oceanography Centre

Important Information

All tide times are corrected for BST where appropriate and are shown in 24 hour clock format. Tidal heights are in metres above Admiralty Chart Datum. This differs from Ordnance Survey datum and the offsets are listed on the tidal statistics page.

Times are shown for High Water (HW) and Low Water (LW), AM and PM for each location. Because the time between tides is normally greater than 12 hours, some mornings and afternoons don't have a tide event and in this case the entry is blank. Very occasionally both tides in a day are within one AM or PM period, and in these cases one may appear in the 'wrong' column - these are all marked with asterisks.

For Blakeney and Wells, only high water predictions are available.

Heights of tides and times of high and low water can vary from the predicted values for many reasons and are particularly affected by weather conditions and, in some areas, river flows. Users are advised to consult with local harbour masters and boatyards and check weather forecasts and warnings before venturing onto the water or walking in exposed coastal areas. Make sure someone ashore knows where you are going and when you are due back.

ALWAYS WEAR A LIFEJACKET ON THE WATER

Published by Bittern Books

A division of Unilake Ltd.

bitternbooks.co.uk

ISBN 978-1-913415-05-1

Printed by Barnwell Print, Aylsham, Norfolk NR11 6SU

All tidal data is computed by POLTIPS software developed at the National Oceanography Centre.

Photographs © Stephen Haines 2021

Bittern Books

Norfolk
Tide Times
2022

Hunstanton ◆ Wells-next-the-Sea
Blakeney ◆ Sheringham
Cromer ◆ Winterton ◆ Gorleston

£2.99